Test Prep Series

GMAT®
Analytical Writing:
Solutions to the Real Argument Topics

60 solved Argument topics with strategies to be used as a benchmark

Expert Strategies and simplified methods to produce focused responses

Scoring Guides for Argument tasks as per the GMAT Guidelines

VIBRANT
PUBLISHERS

GMAT® Analytical Writing:
Solutions to the Real Argument Topics

ISBN-10: 1-946383-57-0

ISBN-13: 978-1-946383-57-0

Library of Congress Control Number: 2012919671

This publication is designed to provide accurate and authoritative information in regard to the subject matter covered. The Author has made every effort in the preparation of this book to ensure the accuracy of the information. However, information in this book is sold without warranty either expressed or implied. The Author or the Publisher will not be liable for any damages caused or alleged to be caused either directly or indirectly by this book.

Vibrant Publishers books are available at special quantity discount for sales promotions, or for use in corporate training programs. For more information please write to **bulkorders@vibrantpublishers.com**

Please email feedback / corrections (technical, grammatical or spelling) to **spellerrors@vibrantpublishers.com**

To access the complete catalogue of Vibrant Publishers, visit **www.vibrantpublishers.com**

Table of Contents

Chapter **1**   **Introduction to the GMAT**   **7**

Chapter **2**   **Analytical Writing Assessment**   **9**

Strategies   9

Scoring Guide   11

Conclusion   12

Chapter **3**   **Solved Argument Tasks with Strategies**   **15**

Argument Task 1 - *The Mercury*   14

Argument Task 2 - *Apogee company*   17

Argument Task 3 - *Financial magazine*   20

Argument Task 4 - *Health club managers*   23

Argument Task 5 - *Cerberus dog food*   26

Argument Task 6 - *Environmental protection*   29

Argument Task 7 - *Big Boards Inc.*   31

Argument Task 8 - *Speedee Airlines*   34

Argument Task 9 - *Corporate newsletter*   36

Argument Task 10 - *Company that makes shampoo*   39

Argument Task 11 - *Olympic Foods*   42

Argument Task 12 - *Large city's council on the arts*   45

Argument Task 13 - *Company manufacturing parts for heavy machinery*   48

Argument Task 14 - *Magazine on trends and lifestyles*   51

Argument Task 15 - *Waymarsh students*   54

Argument Task 16 - *Daily Gazette*   57

Argument Task 17 - *Advertisement for Adams*   60

Argument Task 18 - *Acid-Ease and Pepticaid*   63

Argument Task 19 - *Restaurant industry in Spiessa*   65

Argument Task 20 - *Automobile manufacturing company*   68

Argument Task 21 - *Drug abuse*   71

Argument Task 22 - *City L*   74

Argument Task 23 - *Board to censor movies*   77

Argument Task 24 - *Synthetic Farm Products*   80

Argument Task 25 - *Coffee and cola*   83

Argument Task 26 - *Perks Company*   86

Argument Task 27 - *Fern Valley University*   89

Argument Task 28 - *Professor Taylor*   92

Argument Task 29 - *Avia Airlines*   95

Argument Task 30 - *University hospitals vs community hospitals*   97

Argument Task 31 - *Robin Good*   100

Argument Task 32 - *Recycling of newspaper*   103

Argument Task 33 - *Information technology department of advertising firm*   105

Argument Task 34 - *Excelsior Company*   107

Argument Task 35 - *Government funding of environmental regulatory agencies*   110

Argument Task 36 - *Safer workplace*   113

Argument Task 37 - *West Cambria*   115

Argument Task 38 - *Prime-time television programs*   117

Argument Task 39 - *How to Write a Screenplay for a Movie*   119

Argument Task 40 - *ElectroWares Company*   122

Argument Task 41 - *Tartfish industry*   124

Argument Task 42 - *Advertising spots on KMTV*   126

Argument Task 43 - *Plateau College*   128

Argument Task 44 - *Saluda Consolidated High School*   131

Argument Task 45 - *Books in electronic form*   133

Argument Task 46 - *Take Heart Fitness Center*   136

Argument Task 47 - *Bayview High School*   139

Argument Task 48 - *Store selling gourmet food items*   142

Argument Task 49 - *Ready-to-Ware*   145

Argument Task 50 - *Omnilixir*   148

Argument Task 51 - *Amusement parks*   151

Argument Task 52 - *The Clarion*   153

Argument Task 53 - *Capital Idea - Irongate district*   155

Argument Task 54 - *HuggyBunny*   157

Argument Task 55 - *Exeunt Theater Company*   159

Argument Task 56 - *Capital Idea investment firm - tartfish*   161

Argument Task 57 - *Avia Airlines - commuter route*   163

Argument Task 58 - *GBS Company*   166

Argument Task 59 - *Excel Meats*   168

Argument Task 60 - *Improving services for the city*   171

Dear Student,

Thank you for purchasing **GMAT Analytical Writing: Solutions to the Real Argument Topics.** We are committed to publishing books that are content-rich, concise and approachable enabling more students to read and make the fullest use of them. We hope this book provides the most enriching learning experience as you prepare for your **GRE** exam.

Should you have any questions or suggestions, feel free to email us at **reachus@vibrantpublishers.com**

Thanks again for your purchase. Good luck for your GRE!

- Vibrant Publishers Team

Chapter 1

Introduction to the GMAT

The GMAT is the standardized test required by more than 5200 graduate schools as part of the application package to their business or management programs. Along with your undergraduate transcript, recommendations, work experience, etc., your GMAT scores will determine which college programs will grant you admission. Colleges consider these scores important for two main reasons. First, undergraduate courses and curricula vary from school to school, and second, in the same way that the SAT predicts success in college, the GMAT predicts a student's success in the challenging courses of graduate business and management programs. The higher the score you earn, the more likely you will gain admission to competitive programs at colleges around the country. You can check the websites of desired programs to see the range of scores they consider acceptable as well as the weight they assign to those scores.

The GMAT is composed of four parts: Analytical Writing Assessment, Integrated Reasoning, Quantitative, and Verbal. The test will begin with a 30-minute Analytical Writing Assessment, followed by the 30-minute, 12-question Integrated Reasoning section. Next is the Quantitative portion, made up of 37 questions that you must answer in 75 minutes, and the Verbal portion, made up of 41 questions that also must be answered in 75 minutes.

Even though the test is used for admission to business or management programs, no specific knowledge in these areas is needed to successfully complete the test. All of the information you will need to answer any individual question appears in the question and the answers. The test is computer-adaptive. The degree of difficulty of the questions will change based on your answer history. You will never get many questions that are either too difficult or too easy for you. Your success will derive from your ability to read and follow directions and carefully scrutinize the information in the question or prompt. You will need to read and write in English and have basic math and English skills. The test is delivered in English on a computer, but no special computer skills are needed to complete the test. Basic word processing skills are necessary for composing the essay.

Because the results are important, you should spend some time practicing for the GMAT. At the very least, familiarize yourself with the question formats. Taking one or more practice tests will be most helpful in assuring a high score. Remember that the actual test is timed, so you should time yourself throughout one practice test.

The following strategies will help you complete the GMAT in a timely manner and insure that you get the highest score possible.

a)   Pace yourself; use the allotted time wisely. An on screen clock will keep track of the time remaining and warn you when 5 minutes remain.

b)   Never skim the questions and answers. You may miss important information.

c)   You must confirm the answer you have selected before you can move on to the next question. As long as all of the answers appear on the screen, you can change your answer, but you cannot return to a question you have previously answered.

d)   You cannot skip a question, so, if you are not sure of the answer, eliminate the choices that you can and select the best answer from the choices remaining.

e)   Attempt to finish all of the questions, as leaving several unanswered can have a seriously negative effect on your score.

Chapter **2**

Analytical Writing Assessment

The AWA is the first of four parts of the GMAT, and you will have 30 minutes to plan and type your tessay. You will begin by reading a brief argument in which the author may state a position, make a recommendation, or make a prediction. You may agree or disagree with the author's position, but refrain from stating your own opinion. Your task is to determine how sufficiently the writer has made his case and clearly communicate your critique of the argument in writing. Two independent readers will assign a score between 1 to 6. If their scores are not exact or adjacent, a third reader will evaluate your writing. The readers, who are college professors from a variety of disciplines, will use the following criteria to score your analysis: the overall quality of your ideas; your ability to organize, develop, and express your ideas; your including relevant supporting reasons and examples; and your control of the elements of standard written English.

The following directions appear after each argument, and you should read them carefully.

Discuss how well reasoned you find this argument. In your discussion be sure to analyze the line of reasoning and the use of evidence in the argument. For example, you may need to consider what questionable assumptions underlie the thinking and what alternative explanations or counterexamples might weaken the conclusion. You can also discuss what sort of evidence would strengthen or refute the argument, what changes in the argument would make it more logically sound, and what, if anything, would help you better evaluate its conclusion.

Strategies

While planning your response, focus on the suggestions in the directions. Use the erasable notepad to take notes to help you organize your analysis.

Begin by identifying the audience for the argument. The author may have tailored the information in the argument to this audience, thereby creating some inherent biases. For example, a company's report to its stockholders may include information that makes a company seem more profitable than it really is and omit information that makes stockholders question their investment. A political endorsement will enumerate positive changes that the incumbent has facilitated and point out how his opponent disagrees with that incumbent's policies. An editorial, by its nature, expresses an opinion. Understanding how the audience may influence the type of information included in the argument will help you to single out the questionable assumptions in the argument. The author may have a vested interest in the point of view expressed in the argument. He or she may be a department head in a large company, and provide only positive information about his department's performance designed to insure job security or expansion of his department. Acknowledging hidden agendas will help you evaluate the argument.

Consider the source of the information presented in the argument. The author may cite polls or surveys. Although the survey or poll information may be accurate, it may not actually support the argument. The author may be using survey results to create an analogy, a conclusion drawn by arguing that there are clear similarities between two different events. Be wary of general descriptors like several, some, many, or recent. You should ask, "How many? How recent?"

Next, list the assumptions. Keep in mind that an assumption is not a fact, but it may be based on what appear to be facts in the argument. For example, the writer may say that over the last few years, gold chain sales at Jennie's Jewelry have declined by 20%. A recent survey shows that a significant number of women prefer sterling silver over gold, so Jennie should increase her sterling silver chain inventory to raise her profits. One questionable assumption implied in this statement is that Jennie's sales of gold chain were so high that a 20% reduction has had a big impact on her profits. Another is that Jennie can sell enough sterling silver to compensate for the reduction in gold sales. You might also assume that Jennie has taken no steps to compensate for the reduction in gold sales. The survey results cited here may also lead you to conclude that investing in more sterling silver is a good decision.

The directions tell you to consider alternative explanations or counter examples for the assumptions in the argument. In the case of Jennie's Jewelry, you might think of reasons to explain the 20% decline in gold sales. A new jewelry store may have opened in town. The price of gold may be so high that Jennie bought less of it, and a smaller selection forced customers to shop elsewhere. The higher price may have discouraged customers from purchasing it. Jennie's Jewelry may have experienced an even greater reduction in sterling silver sales. A manufacturer may have closed its plant in Jennie's town, eliminating a significant number of jobs, so all businesses in her town may have suffered losses. If any of these conditions are true, the assumption is faulty. You might be able to draw on your own experience to develop an alternative explanation. It is likely that you live in a town whose independently-owned, small businesses have been affected by the opening of a new mall or big box store, and you can relate the impact of that in your analysis.

What additional information would help you to better evaluate the assumptions? The following pieces of information may help you: the portion of Jennie's total sales that can be attributed to gold jewelry; changes in the price of gold over the last few years; changes in the local economy; what is selling well at Jennie's Jewelry. If you know this information, you can determine if the author's recommendation is reasonable. Try manipulating some numbers that make a 20% decline in gold sales seem either significant or of little concern. For example, consider that gold sales account for 80% of Jennie's total sales. Losing one-fifth of those sales would result in gold sales equaling only 66% of total sales, a significant loss. Sales of other merchandise would have to increase from 20% of the total to 34% of the total. On the other hand, if the sale of gold jewelry accounts for only 10% of total sales for the store, a 20% decline, which would reduce the contribution to 8% of total sales, would be almost negligible.

Making separate lists for the assumptions and/or claims, alternative explanations or counter examples, and missing information will provide a visual aid to assist you in developing your evaluation of any argument. Now, you are prepared to begin composing your evaluation of the argument. You will be able to perform basic word processing functions like cut and paste, so feel free to begin writing about your ideas in any way that is comfortable for you. Some writers complete the introduction before moving on to the body paragraphs, while others prefer to write the introduction after developing their ideas in the body paragraphs. Whatever style suits you, keep in mind the following strategies.

a) Read the argument carefully; reread it as you write to insure that you maintain your focus.

b) Refer to your notes, lists, or outline as you write, but do not hesitate to include ideas that come to you as you write. Your prewriting is just a guide.

c) Fully develop your examples; do not simply list them.

d) In your discussion of alternative explanations or counterexamples, feel free to draw on your own experiences, observations, or readings.

e) Be sure to use a narrative format for your evaluation.

f) Leave some time to reread your response and make any necessary revisions.

g) Keep in mind that you are critiquing the argument, and you may point out both strengths and weaknesses.

Complete enough practice essays to become comfortable with the format. Take as much time as you need with the first few responses, but, eventually, you should complete some practice analyses while timing yourself. Ask someone whose opinion you respect to read some of your analyses and ask him or her to provide constructive feedback. Share the scoring criteria with that person, so he or she can phrase the feedback in the language of the scoring guide.

Scoring Guide

Your goal, after completing practice essays, is to use what you have learned to get the highest score possible on your analysis. In order to earn a score of 6, your analysis must be **Outstanding**. At this level, you will have created a response that demonstrates an insightful analysis of the argument after clearly identifying its important features. Your ideas will be organized logically and be connected with clear transitions to create a cogent response as you provide effective support for your points. Use a variety of sentence structures and apt and accurate vocabulary. Although your writing may have some minor flaws, you should strive for control of the conventions of standard written English, including grammar, usage, and mechanics.

Analyses at score point 5 are described as **Strong**. You have demonstrated the ability to identify the important features of the arguments and analyze them thoughtfully. Your analyses are not formulaic. Your analysis proceeds logically with appropriate transitions between ideas. You demonstrate control of language with sentence variety and appropriate vocabulary. Your response may contain occasional flaws in usage, grammar, and mechanics.

A score point of 4 is for analyses that are considered **Adequate**. You have delivered a competent critique of the argument. You are able to identify and analyze the important features of the argument. You may omit transitions between satisfactorily developed and well- organized ideas. You provide adequate support for the main points in your critique and demonstrate reasonable clarity and sufficient control of language. Although your analysis may have some flaws, your writing generally follows the conventions do standard written English.

Papers that are given a score of 3 are considered to be **Limited**. Although you demonstrate some ability to provide a written analysis of an argument, your flaws are evident. You have failed to identify or analyze most of the important points in the argument. Although some analysis is present, it addresses only tangential or irrelevant matters. Your reasoning is weak. Development of ideas lacks substance, and the organization lacks logic. The analysis may contain either occasional major errors or frequent minor errors in grammar, usage, and mechanics. There is little variety in sentence structure, and sometimes vocabulary is weak or inappropriate.

An analysis assigned a score of 2 is **Seriously Flawed** due to serious weaknesses in analytical writing skills. At this level, your response may state your own opinion on the subject of the argument. If you attempt a critique, you do not develop your ideas or provide relevant support for them. Your response is poorly organized and has serious and frequent errors in sentence structure. Numerous errors in grammar, usage, and mechanics interfere with meaning and coherence.

A **Fundamentally Deficient** analysis earns a score of 1. This paper lacks even the basic skills of analytical writing. Your writing demonstrates the inability to understand the argument, thereby preventing you from identifying important ideas. Any response at this score level has severe and persistent errors in language and sentence structure. The response is virtually incoherent as a result of pervasive errors in grammar, usage, and mechanics.

The final two scoring options are **No Score** and **NR**. Your response will earn a No Score if you simply attempt to copy the prompt, write off topic, write in a language other than English, or write using only keystroke characters. NR is assigned to blank responses.

Conclusion

The Analytical Writing Assessment does not measure the extent of your knowledge about any specific topic or academic content. The argument topics may be about business or any area of general interest. Use your familiarity with the scoring criteria and your practice writing analyses to approach the argument in a manner that displays your ability to think critically about the content of the argument and write your analysis in a thorough and well-developed manner. Express your ideas in an original manner, avoiding formulaic phrases and comparisons.

Chapter **3**

Solved Argument Tasks with Strategies

The following essays and prewriting activities are designed to help the test taker successfully complete the Analytical Writing Assessment portion of the GMAT. To obtain a good score, first determine what the directions are asking you to do. Basically, you must evaluate the strength of an argument. You are not being asked to create an argument or take a position but to analyze the credibility of a position that someone else has taken on an issue. Develop points for your critique by following the suggestions in the directions. Identify any claims and/or assumptions in the argument. This will enable you to create alternative explanations for the conditions that exist in the argument. The argument may need more information to strengthen the author's position. Make a list of additional information that would help you to better evaluate the argument. This list might include questions that you have. As you read the essays, refer to the lists the author has made and notice how development of points in them either weakens or strengthens the argument presented. In the time allotted to craft your essay during the exam, you will not be able to develop each point. Notice that the authors of these essays have selected some points while omitting others. Some essays may include points that do not appear in the prewriting lists. Ideas may come to you as you write, and you should feel free to include them. Just as these authors have done, evaluate how the audience for each argument may affect the content of the argument and the biases inherent in some of them. Use the pattern created here or one that works better for you. However you decide to approach the arguments, practicing will make your essay more coherent and eligible for a high score.

Argument Task 1

> *The following appeared in an announcement issued by the publisher of The Mercury, a weekly newspaper:*
>
> *"Since a competing lower-priced newspaper, The Bugle, was started five years ago, The Mercury's circulation has declined by 10,000 readers. The best way to get more people to read The Mercury is to reduce its price below that of The Bugle, at least until circulation increases to former levels. The increased circulation of The Mercury will attract more businesses to buy advertising space in the paper."*
>
> *Discuss how well reasoned you find this argument. In your discussion be sure to analyze the line of reasoning and the use of evidence in the argument. For example, you may need to consider what questionable Assumptions underlie the thinking and what alternative explanations or counter examples might weaken the conclusion. You can also discuss what sort of evidence would strengthen or refute the argument, what changes in the argument would make it more logically sound, and what, if anything, would help you better evaluate its conclusion.*

Strategies

A good place to start your analysis is by creating a statement that reveals the main idea of the argument. Although the writer is creating an argument, he may ultimately be stating a position, making a recommendation, or making a prediction. It may be helpful for you to determine which of these formats is most evident in the argument.

Recommendation

The publisher should lower the price of *The Mercury* to increase readership and attract more advertisers.

The directions for crafting your response include suggesting that you identify any questionable assumptions that may underlie or support the writer's conclusion. The assumptions may be stated or implied.

Claims and/or Assumptions

a)   The 10,000 readers who no longer read *The Mercury* now read *The Bugle*

b)   *The Bugle*'s circulation is greater than that of *The Mercury*

c)   Readers choose their newspaper based on the price of the paper and will choose the cheapest paper

d)   Businesses choose to advertise in papers with circulations higher than that of *The Mercury*

e)   Other than price, there is no difference between *The Bugle* and *The Mercury*

The author of the argument may have omitted some information to make his position appear stronger. What information would help you decide if the argument has validity or what should the writer's audience know in order to make an informed decision?

Additional information needed to analyze the argument

a) The circulation data for both *The Mercury* and *The Bugle*

b) The difference in price between *The Mercury* and *The Bugle*

c) The cost for advertising in both *The Mercury* and *The Bugle*

d) Information to track the decrease in *The Mercury's* circulation (when did it begin? Is it still declining?)

e) Information about *The Bugle's* circulation. (Is it increasing? Decreasing?)

f) Information about the content of both papers.

g) Information about when *The Bugle* is published. Is it weekly? Daily?

Sample Essay

The author of this recommendation has identified a problem; that the circulation of the weekly newspaper, *The Mercury*, has declined over the last five years. The author claims that this decline is the direct result of the introduction of a lower-priced paper, *The Bugle*, five years ago. He recommends lowering the price of *The Mercury* so that it is less than that of *The Bugle*, which, he believes, will increase readership and attract more advertisers. It may be that the author has accurately identified the cause of *The Mercury's* decline. However, he has made assumptions and omitted key information to support his recommendation.

At the outset, the author assumes that *The Bugle's* readership is greater than that of *The Mercury*, and that the 10,000 readers who no longer buy *The Mercury* now spend their money on *The Bugle*. This may be the case, however, the author has not provided circulation data or other information that would identify why readers are no longer interested in reading *The Mercury* or to prove that *The Bugle's* readership is increasing in correlation to *The Mercury's* decrease. Without this information, there is no way to know what has become of the lost readers of *The Mercury*. They may have moved from the city in a mass exodus due to housing or employment issues. They may now read their news online or rely on television news sources, and see no reason for the additional expense of a newspaper, and it could be that the circulation of both papers is on the decline. If the reason for the loss of readers is anything other than readers choosing a less expensive paper, lowering the price will decrease the company's revenues without increasing circulation.

The author also assumes that other than price, the two newspapers are identical. If *The Bugle* is a daily paper, it may be that readers prefer news that is more current than the weekly paper, *The Mercury*, can provide. If that is the case, reducing the price of *The Mercury* will have no impact, as readers will continue to avoid the stale weekly news in *The Mercury*. It may also be the case that the two papers do not cover the same type of news. Perhaps *The Bugle* is staffed by experienced journalists who provide in-depth reporting of issues that are of great concern for citizens, while *The Mercury* focuses on human interest stories and publishing births, deaths, and anniversaries. If that is the case, those interested in learning more about the issues facing the community will not purchase *The Mercury* now that a hard newspaper is available.

Finally, the author asserts a causal chain: lowering the price of the paper will increase circulation, which will then attract advertisers. He suggests that advertisers are motivated primarily by a newspaper's circulation. If advertisers are motivated by other factors, the potential for increased circulation will not result in additional advertisement sales. The author has not compared advertising rates or presentation between the two papers. Perhaps *The Bugle's* advertising rates are similar to those of *The Mercury*, but ads are presented in full color, or, perhaps, *The Bugle's* rates are less than those of *The Mercury*. Or, perhaps, advertising in newspapers is universally declining and neither paper should expect to increase advertising revenues, as advertisers turn to other media, such as radio and internet marketing.

The publishers of *The Mercury* should review the assumptions made in this memorandum very carefully before taking action. The base assumptions, that *The Bugle* has a greater circulation than *The Mercury*, and that the difference is the direct result of the price difference between the two papers are not evident, and the other claims and recommendations presented fail to make the author's case for lowering the price of *The Mercury*.

Argument Task 2

> *The following appeared in a memorandum from the business department of the Apogee Company:*
>
> *"When the Apogee Company had all its operations in one location, it was more profitable than it is today. Therefore, the Apogee Company should close down its field offices and conduct all its operations from a single location. Such centralization would improve profitability by cutting costs and helping the company maintain better supervision of all employees."*
>
> *Discuss how well reasoned you find this argument. In your discussion be sure to analyze the line of reasoning and the use of evidence in the argument. For example, you may need to consider what questionable Assumptions underlie the thinking and what alternative explanations or counter examples might weaken the conclusion. You can also discuss what sort of evidence would strengthen or refute the argument, what changes in the argument would make it more logically sound, and what, if anything, would help you better evaluate its conclusion.*

Strategies

A good place to start your analysis is by creating a statement that reveals the main idea of the argument. Although the writer is creating an argument, he may ultimately be stating a position, making a recommendation, or making a prediction. It may be helpful for you to determine which of these formats is most evident in the argument.

Recommendation

The company should close all field offices and conduct all business from one location.

The directions for crafting your response include suggesting that you identify any questionable assumptions that may underlie or support the writer's conclusion. The assumptions may be stated or implied.

Claims and/or Assumptions

a) The profitability of the company is directly related to the number of locations the company has.

b) Having multiple locations costs more than having a single location.

c) Having multiple locations makes it difficult to effectively supervise employees.

d) Lack of appropriate supervision of employees has reduced profitability.

e) The company is less profitable now than in the past because of increased expenses, rather than decreased income.

The author of the argument may have omitted some information to make his position appear stronger. What information would help you decide if the argument has validity or what should the writer's audience know in order to make an informed decision?

Additional information needed to analyze the argument

a) For how long have the company's profits been in decline.

b) When did the company initially open additional locations?

c) Information about the company's revenue over the same period (from when there was one location to when there were multiple locations)

d) Information about the company's expenses over the same period (from when there was one location to when there were multiple locations).

e) Information about revenue generated by field offices.

f) Overall market conditions for the company's products.

Sample Essay

The author of this recommendation has identified a problem, that the company is currently less profitable than it was at a time in the past, when it operated from a single office location. The author recommends closing all field offices, which he believes will improve profitability and provide the opportunity for better supervision of employees. It may be that the company is currently less profitable because of increased expenses related to maintaining field offices and decreased efficiency among poorly supervised employees. However, he has made assumptions and omitted key information necessary to support his assertion.

The crux of this argument is that the expense of the field offices is the cause of the decrease in profitability. However, this assumption does not consider the revenue generated by each field office, and the author has not evaluated the relative revenues and expenses of individual offices. It may be that some field offices are not generating enough revenue to offset the expense of maintaining the location. However, it may be that some, if not all field offices, generate significant revenue, above and beyond the cost of the office. Some field offices may be located in areas where it would be impossible to do business without a local branch of the company. Others may be located where it is easy to hire and retain highly specialized and skilled employees who are not easily hired near the company's central location. If either scenario were true, closing these successful field offices could decrease company revenue overall and have a negative impact on the company's profitability. In order to establish the veracity of his argument the author needs to provide more detailed information about the company's profits over time, correlated to the opening of each field office. In addition, he should provide information about individual field offices, noting which are profitable in their own right..

The author further suggests that employees in the field offices are not as well supervised as they might be in a central location. It may be that the author is suggesting that employees who do not receive as much supervision are, as a result, less efficient in completing their work. However, he has not made that point explicitly. It may be that employees in the field offices do receive less supervision, but that they are more motivated to complete their work because they appreciate the autonomy they are afforded, and, it may be that employees in a central location, who are closely supervised, resent being micromanaged, and, knowing that their work will be checked and rechecked, are less meticulous about the work they produce. The author should provide more information about the effects of different levels of supervision on employee productivity and the quality of work produced. Without this information, the comment about supervision is not relevant to the argument he is making.

Finally, there may be market factors that are affecting the company's profitability. It may be that the cost of raw materials has increased, that market conditions have required a price drop, or that recent competition has made the company's products less attractive to customers. The author of this recommendation writes from a position of considering only one possible cause of the decline, and if that decline is not at all related to the expenses of field offices, closing those offices could eliminate opportunities to reach new customers and increase revenue.

The executives of Apogee Company should review this recommendation and consider other data before moving forward. Jumping to the same conclusions as the author, and rushing to centralize the company's operations may increase profitability, but without additional information, there is no way to know if that will be the case.

Argument Task 3

> *The following appeared in the opinion column of a financial magazine:*
>
> *"On average, middle-aged consumers devote 39 percent of their retail expenditure to department store products and services, while for younger consumers the average is only 25 percent. Since the number of middle-aged people will increase dramatically within the next decade, department stores can expect retail sales to increase significantly during that period. Furthermore, to take advantage of the trend, these stores should begin to replace some of those products intended to attract the younger consumer with products intended to attract the middle-aged consumer."*
>
> *Discuss how well reasoned you find this argument. In your discussion be sure to analyze the line of reasoning and the use of evidence in the argument. For example, you may need to consider what questionable Assumptions underlie the thinking and what alternative explanations or counter examples might weaken the conclusion. You can also discuss what sort of evidence would strengthen or refute the argument, what changes in the argument would make it more logically sound, and what, if anything, would help you better evaluate its conclusion.*

Strategies

A good place to start your analysis is by creating a statement that reveals the main idea of the argument. Although the writer is creating an argument, he may ultimately be stating a position, making a recommendation, or making a prediction. It may be helpful for you to determine which of these formats is most evident in the argument.

Recommendation

Department stores should anticipate the growing population of middle-aged shoppers by replacing products intended for younger consumers with those that will attract middle-aged consumers.

The directions for crafting your response include suggesting that you identify any questionable assumptions that may underlie or support the writer's conclusion. The assumptions may be stated or implied.

Claims and/or Assumptions

   a) Total retail expenditures of middle aged and younger consumers are equal so that 39% of middle aged retail expenditures is greater than 25% of younger consumer expenditures.

   b) The percentage of retail spending done in department stores will remain static into the future, so that consumers will continue to spend money in the next decade as they currently do.

   c) There is a significant difference in the types of products of interest to middle-aged and younger consumers.

   d) By replacing products that attract younger consumers with those that attract middle aged consumers now, department stores will appeal to older consumers in the next decade.

The author of the argument may have omitted some information to make his position appear stronger. What information would help you decide if the argument has validity or what should the writer's audience know in order to make an informed decision?

Additional information needed to analyze the argument

a) Average total amount of money spent on retail expenditures by middle-aged consumers

b) Average total amount of money spent on retail expenditures by younger consumers

c) Information on spending trends currently, such as what retail venues might be experiencing a trend of increased expenditures over time.

d) Information to show that retail expenditures in department stores have either remained steady or increased in the last ten years.

e) Information about the types of products that appeal to middle aged consumers

f) Information about the types of products that appeal to younger consumers

Sample Essay

Based on data measuring population trends and information about the retail expenditures of people of different ages, the author proposes reevaluating inventory of department stores to better accommodate the unique tastes of middle-aged shoppers, whom, he claims will spend more money than younger consumers in the next ten years. It may be that middle-aged shoppers will become the most active department-store spenders in the next decade, and that this recommendation is insightful of future trends. However, the author has made potentially flawed assumptions about the information he has, and, as a result, has made a recommendation based on predictions that may not be accurate.

First, the author begins by comparing the retail expenditures of middle-aged and younger consumers. To support his recommendation the author assumes that both groups of shoppers allot the same amount of money toward retail expenditures, so that 39 % of middle aged expenditures is greater than 25% of younger shopper's expenditures. However, that may not be the case. For example, it may be that younger shoppers, who may live with their parents or with roommates, and who are attracted to trends and fads, may allot up to $1000 per month toward retail expenditures. Middle-aged shoppers, on the other hand, may have other expenses, such as home mortgages, college tuition, and health insurance, and therefore choose to allot just $100 per month to retail expenditures. In this scenario, younger shoppers would, on average, spend $250 per month in department stores, while middle aged shoppers would spend just $39. To bolster his recommendation, the author should include data on the average dollar amount spent on retail expenditures by each age group.

Further, the author's recommendation is dependent on the idea that as the population of middle-aged people increases, the percent of their retail expenditures spent in department stores will remain unchanged. If, as the population ages, new and more convenient forms of commerce emerge, such as more robust online shopping experiences, or if an economic downturn within the next ten years limits the disposable incomes of people in this population group, the author's claim will not hold true, as they may spend less money in department stores than people of similar age did ten years earlier.

Another point that is crucial to the author's claim is the notion that middle-aged shoppers and younger shoppers seek vastly different products, so that a department store that caters primarily to younger shoppers will have little to offer those who are middle aged. Without information about the types of products most often purchased in department stores, this point does not hold true. For example, it could be that department stores are the primary shopping venue for those of any age seeking wardrobe staples, such as athletic shoes, underwear, or basics such as white shirts and khaki pants. If most shoppers choose department stores for these, regardless of age, the aging population may not change types of products shoppers buy in department stores.

Finally, the author recommends changing store inventory now to accommodate older shoppers that may purchase from department stores in the future. If department stores are currently profiting from selling products to younger customers, and, if the growth in old shoppers does hold true, it will not be for several years. Changing the inventory may result in decreasing expenditures from younger shoppers and result in no change in purchases from those who are middle-aged.

While the author's recommendations may hold true, the author has not provided enough data to support his opinion, and action taken based on this passage may not yield the desired results. If department stores follow this advice without further information, they may risk seeing a decline in sales currently and in years to come.

Argument Task 4

The following appeared as part of an article in a health club trade publication:

"After experiencing a decline in usage by its members, Healthy Heart fitness center built an indoor pool. Since usage did not increase significantly, it appears that health club managers should adopt another approach - lowering membership fees rather than installing expensive new features."

Discuss how well reasoned you find this argument. In your discussion be sure to analyze the line of reasoning and the use of evidence in the argument. For example, you may need to consider what questionable Assumptions underlie the thinking and what alternative explanations or counter examples might weaken the conclusion. You can also discuss what sort of evidence would strengthen or refute the argument, what changes in the argument would make it more logically sound, and what, if anything, would help you better evaluate its conclusion.

Strategies

A good place to start your analysis is by creating a statement that reveals the main idea of the argument. Although the writer is creating an argument, he may ultimately be stating a position, making a recommendation, or making a prediction. It may be helpful for you to determine which of these formats is most evident in the argument.

Recommendation

Fitness centers should not spend money on swimming pools or other expensive new features, but, rather, should lower membership fees to attract members.

The directions for crafting your response include suggesting that you identify any questionable assumptions that may underlie or support the writer's conclusion. The assumptions may be stated or implied.

Claims and/or Assumptions

a) The number of members who joined Healthy Heart fitness because of the pool was less than those who might join if there were no pool but the cost was lower.

b) Those who joined Healthy Heart after the pool installation were not specifically motivated to do so by the pool.

c) All fitness centers are similar to Healthy Heart

d) All potential fitness center members are similar to those who considered Healthy Heart

e) The decline in Healthy Heart membership prior to the installation of the pool had nothing to do with the availability of an indoor pool.

f) If Healthy Heart and other fitness centers decrease membership fees, membership will increase.

The author of the argument may have omitted some information to make his position appear stronger. What

information would help you decide if the argument has validity or what should the writer's audience know in order to make an informed decision?

Additional information needed to analyze the argument

a)   Information from exit surveys to show why Healthy Heart members left the fitness club.

b)   Information about new customers who joined after the installation of the Healthy Heart pool, indicating why new members joined.

c)   Information about other health clubs, including features, membership fees, and membership.

d)   Healthy Heart's marketing efforts, including awareness in the community of its features.

e)   The actual increase of membership that followed the installation of the pool.

Sample Essay

Based on the membership trends of one health club, Healthy Heart fitness center, the author of this trade article argues that all health clubs should consider lower membership fees, in lieu of adding expensive features. Specifically, he argues that lowering membership fees will result in a greater increase in membership than adding new, expensive features such as indoor swimming pools. While there may be some validity to the notion that potential health club members consider fees when choosing a health club, this claim makes several assumptions not supported with evidence.

The article begins with flawed analysis of a series of events. Healthy Heart health club experienced a decline in membership. To reverse this trend the club installed an indoor pool. The resulting increase in membership, according to the author, was insignificant. First, it is not clear what the author means when he says the increase in membership was insignificant. It could mean that it was not enough to offset the cost of the pool, that the increase was not equal to the decline that preceded it, or that it did not meet the target increase set prior to the pool installation. It is also not clear what caused the initial decline. Did members leave for newer, better equipped clubs? Was there an economic downturn in the area that made any health club membership too expensive? Was there a recent sale on home-based exercise equipment that encouraged people to begin exercising at home? Without specific information about the initial decline and the resulting increase, there is no way for the reader to determine the relevance of this information to the argument made by the author.

Second, the author assumes that since there has not been significant growth in membership following the installation of the pool, potential members are not interested in any expensive features in health clubs and can only be enticed to join by lower membership fees. It may be that potential members are not interested in an indoor pool, but that is not evidence that other features will not encourage them to join. For example, some members may be interested in spin classes, featuring state of the art stationary bicycles, and will only consider clubs that offer this equipment. It may be that the pool Healthy Heart installed was small, not heated, or not conducive to the types of exercise potential clients were interested in. Without more information there is no evidence to show that a lack of interest in the club's pool equates to a lack of interest in all expensive equipment installations.

The author also makes the assumption that the experience of Healthy Heart health club can be extended to all health clubs. This assumption is the basis of his argument. While it might be the case that the expensive indoor pool did little to increase membership at Healthy Heart, there is no way to extrapolate this data to suggest similar results can be applied universally. It may be that Healthy Heart is located in a warm part of the country where many people have their own pools or have year-round access to a beach. Landlocked regions in colder climates might be more likely to experience an uptick in membership as potential customers would see the pool as a benefit they could not find elsewhere. More information is needed about the location, climate, and general customer base of Healthy Heart, and then, perhaps the results could be extended to apply to other similar clubs in similar locations.

Finally, the author makes the claim that since the pool installation did little to increase membership, the only other option is to decrease membership fees. This claim is based on the idea that an indoor pool is somehow representative of all expensive health club features, and that if one is not a draw for customers, no other feature will be either. There is no information about Healthy Heart's current membership fees and how they compare to those of other health clubs in the region. If Healthy Heart's fees are significantly more, then price may be a factor in membership recruitment. However, if Healthy Heart's fees are similar to or lower than those of other, more popular clubs, lowering fees is unlikely to have any effect. Applying this approach to all clubs is unlikely to yield membership increases, as there is no information about the average fees correlated to membership. In order to make this claim the author must provide more data about health club fee structures and how they are correlated to overall membership.

The author of this article obviously intended to provide a strategy for struggling health clubs to increase membership. However, because of the flawed assumptions made and the lack of required data, this recommendation should not be followed as there is no indication it will lead to membership growth.

Argument Task 5

The following appeared in the promotional literature for Cerberus dog food:

"Obesity is a great problem among pet dogs, just as it is among their human owners. Obesity in humans is typically caused by consuming more calories than the body needs. For humans, a proper diet for losing weight is a reduced-calorie diet that is high in fiber and carbohydrates but low in fat. Therefore, the best way for dog owners to help their dogs lose weight in a healthy way is to restrict the dog's diet to Cerberus reduced calorie dog food, which is high in fiber and carbohydrates but low in fat."

Discuss how well reasoned you find this argument. In your discussion be sure to analyze the line of reasoning and the use of evidence in the argument. For example, you may need to consider what questionable Assumptions underlie the thinking and what alternative explanations or counter examples might weaken the conclusion. You can also discuss what sort of evidence would strengthen or refute the argument, what changes in the argument would make it more logically sound, and what, if anything, would help you better evaluate its conclusion.

Strategies

A good place to start your analysis is by creating a statement that reveals the main idea of the argument. Although the writer is creating an argument, he may ultimately be stating a position, making a recommendation, or making a prediction. It may be helpful for you to determine which of these formats is most evident in the argument.

Recommendation

Dog owners should feed their dogs Cerberus dog food because it is the same high fiber and carbohydrate, low fat, diet formula that helps humans lose weight.

The directions for crafting your response include suggesting that you identify any questionable assumptions that may underlie or support the writer's conclusion. The assumptions may be stated or implied.

Claims and/or Assumptions

a) The cause of obesity in humans is the same as the cause of obesity in dogs.

b) The weight-loss diet that works for humans will be effective for dogs.

c) Cerberus dog food has fewer calories than typical dog food.

d) A diet high in fiber and carbohydrates is lower in calories than other diets.

e) There is no other way to combat obesity other than diet changes.

f) Diet restrictions for dogs will have no adverse effects and only result in weight loss.

g) All breeds of dogs are alike in their dietary needs and causes of obesity.

The author of the argument may have omitted some information to make his position appear stronger. What

information would help you decide if the argument has validity or what should the writer's audience know in order to make an informed decision?

Additional information needed to analyze the argument

a) The number of calories a dog typically uses in normal activity.

b) The basic nutritional requirements of dogs.

c) Other causes of obesity that may not be typical.

Sample Essay

The author begins with the well-known assertion that obesity is on the rise in both humans and pet dogs. He then summarizes the cause and one way to address obesity in humans and asserts that the obesity in dogs is the result of the same cause and can be treated in the same way. The author's interest in addressing a serious health problem in pet dogs is laudable, but his argument is based solely on his limited knowledge of obesity in humans, and there is no evidence the same solution will apply to dogs.

First of all, the author begins with the assertion that obesity results when more calories are consumed than are needed. The author, however, does not expand on the idea of a calorie imbalance causing obesity. He transitions directly into a description of a human diet change that can result in weight loss: one that is higher in fiber and carbohydrates and lower in fat. However, if this arguably healthier diet is not lower in calories and no change is made to body's need for calories, such as an increase in exercise, there is no reason to believe this diet will effectively reduce either a dog's or, for that matter, a human's weight. The author must consider including information about typical calorie requirements for dogs and humans, as well as the calorie value of the suggested diet.

As concerning as the lack of information about calorie content is the author's assumption that the dietary needs of dogs and humans are similar. While the high-fiber, high-carb, low-fat diet approach may be successful in reducing weight in humans, there is no way to know if this diet will be effective, or even healthy for dogs. It may be that dogs require a diet high in protein and fat to maintain their body systems, and that, further, their nutritional needs are far different from those of humans. Relegating a dog to a human diet, high in carbohydrates and fiber may, in this case result in weight loss, but only as an effect of malnutrition, since the dog will not be receiving the food it needs to maintain good health. More information is needed about the specific nutritional needs of dogs before this recommendation can be considered valid or even safe for animals.

In addition, the author appears to assume that the main reason for obesity in dogs is due to the diet which provides more calories than dogs need. The inverse may be true, in that pet dogs may not typically have access to adequate exercise opportunities, in which case, their diets may be appropriate, but they are not expending enough energy to maintain good health. The author must include veterinary recommendations for exercise for typical breeds of dogs and information about the amount of exercise dogs typically engage in before this recommendation can be considered valid.

Finally, the author assumes that all dog breeds are identical in terms of nutritional needs and obesity in all breeds can be addressed in the same way. Anyone who has seen a Chihuahua side by side with a Great Dane understands that dog breeds are extremely varied. Smaller breeds may have nutritional needs lesser than much larger dogs, and applying a one-solution-fits-all plan for canine weight loss may result in adverse effects.

The author's recommendation, while well-intended, is not well supported and is based on several potentially flawed assumptions. In order to strengthen this recommendation the author must provide additional information to support the claims he's made.

Argument Task 6

> *The following appeared in an editorial from a magazine produced by an organization dedicated to environmental protection:*
>
> *"In order to effectively reduce the amount of environmental damage that industrial manufacturing plants cause, those who manage the plants must be aware of the specific amount and types of damage caused by each of their various manufacturing processes. However, few corporations have enough financial incentive to monitor this information. In order to guarantee that corporations reduce the damage caused by their plants, the federal government should require every corporation to produce detailed annual reports on the environmental impact of their manufacturing process, and the government should impose stiff financial penalties for failure to produce these reports."*
>
> *Discuss how well reasoned you find this argument. In your discussion be sure to analyze the line of reasoning and the use of evidence in the argument. For example, you may need to consider what questionable Assumptions underlie the thinking and what alternative explanations or counter examples might weaken the conclusion. You can also discuss what sort of evidence would strengthen or refute the argument, what changes in the argument would make it more logically sound, and what, if anything, would help you better evaluate its conclusion.*

Strategies

A good place to start your analysis is by creating a statement that reveals the main idea of the argument. Although the writer is creating an argument, he may ultimately be stating a position, making a recommendation, or making a prediction. It may be helpful for you to determine which of these formats is most evident in the argument.

Recommendation

The government should require that manufacturing plants file detailed reports of environmental damage caused by their plants in order to decrease environmental damage.

The directions for crafting your response include suggesting that you identify any questionable assumptions that may underlie or support the writer's conclusion. The assumptions may be stated or implied.

Claims and/or Assumptions

  a) Being aware of environmental damage caused by industrial manufacturing will lead to a decrease in environmental damage caused by industrial manufacturing.

  b) Requiring reports on environmental damage is the same as decreasing environmental damage.

  c) The cause of environmental damage is poor reporting practices.

  d) Manufacturers will file reports that are thorough and honest.

  e) Manufacturers do not currently monitor environmental damage

f)   The reason manufacturers do not currently monitor environmental damage is there is no financial incentive to do so.

g)   The cost of fines for not filing environmental reports will be greater than the expense of compiling and submitting the reports.

The author of the argument may have omitted some information to make his position appear stronger. What information would help you decide if the argument has validity or what should the writer's audience know in order to make an informed decision?

Additional information needed to analyze the argument

a)   Current reporting practices of industrial manufacturers

b)   The cost of creating the report the author proposes.

c)   The cost of fines for companies that do not submit reports.

d)   The types of environmental damage caused by industrial manufacturers.

e)   The process the government will use to test the accuracy of the filed reports.

Sample Essay

The author of this editorial clearly cares about the impact of industrial manufacturing on the environment, and has written an editorial suggesting a means of ensuring manufacturers are held responsible for the damage they do to the environment, which he believes will lead to a decrease in environmental impact. While the intent of the recommendation is laudable, the author has made several assumptions and omitted key information that might show it would be effective.

The crux of the author's recommendation is the notion that compelling companies to write detailed reports on the environmental damage caused by their manufacturing activities will in some way lead to a reduction in environmental damage. He further suggests that requiring the filing of these reports by threatening stiff financial penalties will ensure that the documentation is complete and filed in a timely fashion. However, reporting environmental damage is not the same as reducing environmental damage. Nowhere in this recommendation is there any suggestion that companies will be penalized for polluting or otherwise damaging the environment. Rather, the only penalty noted is for failing to produce the report on time. So, in theory, a manufacturer could pollute rivers, forests, and parklands with toxic waste year after year, and face no penalty whatsoever, as long as the pollution were recorded in a report submitted to the federal government by the established due dates. In order for this recommendation to fulfill the author's intent of reducing pollution it must include some penalty or sanction related to the actual pollution, and not only to the timely record keeping of the polluting activities.

This recommendation also assumes that no such reporting mechanism is currently in place, and that manufacturers are currently not held accountable for reporting their environmental impact. If that is not the case, and if companies already file reports on environmental damage with the federal government, this recommendation offers no change to the current procedure, and would not be likely to affect any change in the damage caused by industrial manufacturing. To support his argument the author should include information about current reporting requirements and how his recommendation improves upon those requirements.

Another point the author has not considered is the possibility that manufacturers may compile reports that are incomplete or inaccurate. This recommendation does not suggest that companies will face penalties for filing reports that are not 100% accurate. Companies could simply lie about the environmental damage caused by their companies, and, as long as they file the reports on time, face no penalties. In order to support his goal of reducing environmental damage the author should devise some means of auditing reports to ensure accuracy so that the information submitted is a true representation of the companies' actions.

Finally, the author believes companies will be motivated to submit the required reports by the threat of stiff penalties. He has, however, neglected to consider the cost companies will incur in producing these reports. If companies determine that the cost of recording and reporting environmental damage is greater than the fines they would face if they neglected to do so, it is likely that many would simply fail to submit the information, pay the fine, and continue on with the current business practices. To make this reporting procedure truly mandatory, the author should develop some means of compelling compliance that is certain to lead to all companies filing the reports.

The author's intent is commendable, and most readers would agree that protecting the environment from damage caused by industrial manufacturing should be a priority; however, there is no evidence that this recommendation will fulfill that goal. The author should revisit the assumptions that drive the recommendation and consider additional information necessary to create a relevant and effective proposal.

Argument Task 7

> *The following is from a campaign by Big Boards Inc. to convince companies in River City that their sales will increase if they use Big Boards billboards for advertising their locally manufactured products:*
>
> *"The potential of Big Boards to increase sales of your products can be seen from an experiment we conducted last year. We increased public awareness of the name of the current national women's marathon champion by publishing her picture and her name on billboards in River City for a period of three months. Before this time, although the champion had just won her title and was receiving extensive national publicity, only five percent of 15,000 randomly surveyed residents of River City could correctly name the champion when shown her picture; after the three-month advertising experiment, 35 percent of respondents from a second survey could supply her name."*
>
> *Discuss how well reasoned you find this argument. In your discussion be sure to analyze the line of reasoning and the use of evidence in the argument. For example, you may need to consider what questionable Assumptions underlie the thinking and what alternative explanations or counter examples might weaken the conclusion. You can also discuss what sort of evidence would strengthen or refute the argument, what changes in the argument would make it more logically sound, and what, if anything, would help you better evaluate its conclusion.*

Strategies

A good place to start your analysis is by creating a statement that reveals the main idea of the argument. Although the writer is creating an argument, he may ultimately be stating a position, making a recommendation, or making a prediction. It may be helpful for you to determine which of these formats is most evident in the argument.

Recommendation

Sales of a company's products will be increased by publishing pictures of the product on billboards in River City.

The directions for crafting your response include suggesting that you identify any questionable assumptions that may underlie or support the writer's conclusion. The assumptions may be stated or implied.

Claims and/or Assumptions

a) Awareness of the marathon champion as a direct result of the billboards

b) Name recognition is increased by posting images on billboards

c) Awareness of products can be increased in the same way as awareness of a champion sports star

d) Name recognition of a product equates to an increase in product sales

e) The national publicity the marathon champion received did not affect her name recognition among the surveyed residents.

f)   Respondents of the first and second surveys were identical

The author of the argument may have omitted some information to make his position appear stronger. What information would help you decide if the argument has validity or what should the writer's audience know in order to make an informed decision?

Additional information needed to analyze the argument

a)   Data to show a causal effect of name recognition on product sales.

b)   Information about the two groups of respondents surveyed.

c)   Data to show the impact of national publicity on name recognition of the marathon champion.

d)   Timing of the national publicity for the marathon champion relative to the placement of billboards.

Sample Essay

In an ambitious sales campaign, Big Boards, Inc. claims that exposure via their company's billboards will raise awareness of a client's product by 30 percent within just three months, and that the raised awareness of the product will result in increased sales. The company's claim is based exclusively on the results of a name recognition study Big Boards, Inc. conducted relative to a national women's marathon champion. The claim of this sales proposal is based on several assumptions and lacks relevant data. So, while exposure via Big Boards billboards may have some effect on product sales, there is no way to determine that outcome based on the evidence provided.

The main claim in this proposal relies on the notion that Big Board billboards were responsible for raising public awareness of a national champion marathon runner. The author notes that when the billboards bearing the runner's image were first erected she had just been named champion. In the three months that the billboards remained posted around the city the champion also received national publicity for her achievement. Although the author claims that the billboards were the cause of the significant increase in awareness of the marathon runner's achievements, it is just as likely that during the three months the billboards were in place the residents saw the marathon runner on television interviews, magazine covers, and on the internet. There is no evidence that the billboards, specifically led to the increased awareness.

Even if Big Boards billboards could somehow prove that their billboards were the only reason people became aware of the marathon champion, there is no evidence to support their claim that increased awareness will lead to increased sales. What, if anything, was sold through the increased awareness of the marathon champion's achievements? Without evidence that the public's awareness of who the champion was could be tied to some purchasing action, such as buying action figures, fitness wear, or other some product, this claim cannot reasonably be made.

Finally, even if readers accept that Big Board billboards raise awareness, and that the raised awareness could result increased sales, the author would have to provide some evidence to show that the net increase in revenue created by these sales would offset the cost of the billboards for this to be a reasonable proposal. That is, if raising awareness by 30% in fact led to raising sales by 30%, the author would have to show evidence that a 30% increase in sales would be more than the cost of the billboards. If, for example, a candy company which had an average monthly revenue of $10,000 per month decided to advertise on several billboards throughout River City at a cost of $5,000 per month, and, as a result, saw an increase in sales of 30% or $3,000 per month, the company would experience a net loss of $2,000 per month. Without more information, it is not clear what companies could, potentially, benefit from this type of advertising.

While billboard advertising may be an effective means of raising product awareness, and might even, in some cases lead to increased sales, this proposal does not support either claim. The author has made broad assumptions about the effects of the billboards and has not included relevant information necessary to prove his point.

Argument Task 8

The following appeared in an article in a travel magazine:

"After the airline industry began requiring airlines to report their on-time rates, Speedee Airlines achieved the number one on-time rate, with more than 89 percent of its flights arriving on time each month. And now Speedee is offering more flights to more destinations than ever before. Clearly, Speedee is the best choice for today's business traveler."

Discuss how well reasoned you find this argument. In your discussion be sure to analyze the line of reasoning and the use of evidence in the argument. For example, you may need to consider what questionable Assumptions underlie the thinking and what alternative explanations or counter examples might weaken the conclusion. You can also discuss what sort of evidence would strengthen or refute the argument, what changes in the argument would make it more logically sound, and what, if anything, would help you better evaluate its conclusion.

Strategies

A good place to start your analysis is by creating a statement that reveals the main idea of the argument. Although the writer is creating an argument, he may ultimately be stating a position, making a recommendation, or making a prediction. It may be helpful for you to determine which of these formats is most evident in the argument.

Recommendation

Business travelers should choose Speedee Airlines because the company has the top on-time rate, and Speedee flies to more destinations than ever before.

The directions for crafting your response include suggesting that you identify any questionable assumptions that may underlie or support the writer's conclusion. The assumptions may be stated or implied.

Claims and/or Assumptions

a) Speedee airlines has maintained its on-time rate since immediately after being required to report these statistics.

b) Other airlines have not increased their on-time rates to surpass that of Speedee Airlines.

c) Speedee Airlines on-time rate reflects on-time flights throughout all its routes.

d) Speedee Airlines flies to many destinations, most of which are of interest to business travelers.

The author of the argument may have omitted some information to make his position appear stronger. What information would help you decide if the argument has validity or what should the writer's audience know in order to make an informed decision?

Additional information needed to analyze the argument

a) Speedee Airlines current on-time rates

b) On-time rates of all airlines flying the same routes as Speedee Airlines.

c) The current cities Speedee Airlines services, and how these have changed over time.

d) The most desirable airline routes for business travelers.

e) Information about on-time rates for specific routes Speedee Airlines travels.

Sample Essay

This travel magazine article clearly recommends that business travelers choose Speedee Airlines because of the airline's superior on-time rates and because it has increased its number of flights and the number of destinations it serves. The author has made several assumptions in making this argument and has neglected to include key information that would show it to be true.

First, the fact that at a time in the past, when airlines were first required to report on-time rates, Speedee Airlines was at the top with 89% of its flights on time is laudable. However, the author neglects to note how long ago this was, the on-time rates reported by other airlines, and if these statistics have changed in the time since reporting was first required. This additional information could demonstrate if this statistic is irrelevant. For example, if the initial reporting requirement occurred ten years ago, and since then Speedee's on-time rate has declined to 50% while the rates of Swift Airlines and Quicklee Airlines have increased to 90% and 95% respectively, there would be no reason to choose Speedee airline for a route currently serviced by either of these two airlines. In addition, if at the time of reporting, there were multiple airlines ranked at "the top" with 89% on-time flights, there would be no reason to believe that Speedee Airlines was superior in efficient service.

If, in fact, Speedee was the only airline ranked at the top for on-line service, and if it has maintained that rate, and no other airlines have surpassed this statistic, there still is not enough information to determine Speedee is the best choice for business travelers. Speedee may experience 100% on time rates for some destinations, such as short trips from smaller regional airports to remote vacation destinations on flights that are run several times a day, but on longer, less frequent flights to cities typically considered business centers, experience long delays and flight cancellations, making it impractical to rely on Speedee for reliable travel to these cities. The statistic alone does not demonstrate service that would appeal to business travelers, and more information is required to demonstrate on-time travel to the most desirable cities for business travelers.

The author also notes that Speedee Airlines now offers more flights to more destinations than ever before, which gives the reader the impression that the airline maintains a wide range of routes with frequent flights. However, there is no point of comparison. If, in the past, Speedee served two cities with two flights daily and now serves three cities, with three flights daily, it does, indeed serve more cities and offer more flights than ever before, but its routes and availability of flights remain limited. Even if Speedee has a more typical number of routes and flights, the addition of more routes and flights is not necessarily a benefit for business travelers. If, for example, Speedee flies from multiple mid-western cities to multiple vacation destinations such as Orlando, Cancun, and the Bahamas, but offers no flights at all to New York, Los Angeles, or Chicago, the additional routes and flights would be of little benefit to typical business travelers. The author must provide specific details about the routes, cities served, and number of flights daily to support this point.

The author of this article is enthusiastic about Speedee Airlines, but his enthusiasm may be misplaced. Without additional information to support his assumptions and data to support his claims, this cannot be considered a meaningful recommendation for business travelers.

Argument Task 9

> *The following appeared in the editorial section of a corporate newsletter:*
>
> *"The common notion that workers are generally apathetic about management issues is false, or at least outdated: a recently published survey indicates that 79 percent of the nearly 1,200 workers who responded to survey questionnaires expressed a high level of interest in the topics of corporate restructuring and redesign of benefits programs."*
>
> *Discuss how well reasoned you find this argument. In your discussion be sure to analyze the line of reasoning and the use of evidence in the argument. For example, you may need to consider what questionable Assumptions underlie the thinking and what alternative explanations or counter examples might weaken the conclusion. You can also discuss what sort of evidence would strengthen or refute the argument, what changes in the argument would make it more logically sound, and what, if anything, would help you better evaluate its conclusion.*

Strategies

A good place to start your analysis is by creating a statement that reveals the main idea of the argument. Although the writer is creating an argument, he may ultimately be stating a position, making a recommendation, or making a prediction. It may be helpful for you to determine which of these formats is most evident in the argument.

Recommendation

The reader should subscribe to the common notion that workers are generally apathetic about management issues such as changes to benefits plans and corporate restructuring, as evidence shows that is not the case.

The directions for crafting your response include suggesting that you identify any questionable assumptions that may underlie or support the writer's conclusion. The assumptions may be stated or implied.

Claims and/or Assumptions

a) The idea that workers are not interested in management issues is outdated, or that they were not interested in these issues at some time in the past.

b) The 1,200 workers surveyed are representative of the entire workforce of the region.

c) Workers are interested in issues related to corporate restructuring and redesign of benefits programs because they care about the impact of these issues on the corporations.

d) Respondents consider these issues, management issues, and not employee issues

e) Respondents were candid in their responses on the survey.

f) Respondents were not engaged in management roles

The author of the argument may have omitted some information to make his position appear stronger. What information would help you decide if the argument has validity or what should the writer's audience know in order to make an informed decision?

Additional information needed to analyze the argument

a) Information from prior surveys on this issue, to show that there is, in fact an increase in interest.

b) Information about the positions and job titles held by respondents.

c) Information about the delivery of the surveys, including confidentiality or anonymity of responses.

d) The total number of surveys distributed and what percentage were returned.

e) Details about wording and presentation of questions on the survey.

Sample Essay

The author of this editorial makes the claim that the "common notion" that workers are generally apathetic about management issues is false, or at least outdated," based on the results of a survey completed by 1,200 workers. While these results, that 79% of respondents are concerned with issues such as corporate restructuring and redesign of benefits programs may indicate employee interest in management issues, the author has not provided enough information to confirm that is the case.

The author of this claim has made several assumptions in developing the claim, many of which are not supported. First, he begins from the position that there is a "common notion" that some topics typically considered management issues are of little or no interest to workers. However, there is no evidence of prior surveys or any other evidence that this "notion" has been held in the past or if it was widely held. Therefore, there is no way to show that this survey indicates significantly more interest in these issues than existed at some time in the past.

Another assumption made by this author is that the 1,200 workers surveyed are representative of all workers. If, for example, the majority of workers surveyed are those who aspire to management positions or were, at the time of the survey, in management training programs, the responses they provided would be different from workers with no management experience or aspirations, and would, therefore produce results that are not representative of all workers. Furthermore, even if the workers who responded were not engaged in or aspiring to management roles, there is no information about the setting of survey. It could be that workers were closely supervised while completing the surveys, and felt compelled to answer in a way that appeared to be supportive of their employer, even if those answers were not reflective of their own opinions. To further bolster the author's claim, more information about the sample and the context of the survey should be provided.

Even if the survey were given primarily to workers with no management aspirations, and if the context were conducive to candid answers from these workers, the issues noted, changes to the company's organization and to the benefits offered to employees, are not of interest exclusively to those in management. Workers might be interested in information about corporate restructuring, for example, because restructuring activities can lead to downsizing and layoffs of workers. Similarly, restructuring benefits programs would likely have a direct impact on workers, including health insurance, vacation, and retirement programs, all of which are topics that are of great concern to all workers, and not only to those in management. The author of this claim would better be able to support his stance if he were to survey workers on issues that clearly interested only those in management, such as executive profit sharing or long term expansion planning.

Finally, the author notes that 1,200 surveys were returned, but does not indicate how many were distributed. If, for example, surveys were distributed to 12,000 workers, but only 1,200 responded, that would indicate that 90% of those who received the survey were not interested in responding, thus supporting the "common notion that workers are generally apathetic about management issues."

Overall, this is an interesting claim, but the author has not provided the details and data necessary to show it to be true.

Argument Task 10

> *The following appeared in a memorandum from the president of a company that makes shampoo:*
>
> *"A widely publicized study claims that HR2, a chemical compound in our shampoo, can contribute to hair loss after prolonged use. This study, however, involved only 500 subjects. Furthermore, we have received no complaints from our customers during the past year, and some of our competitors actually use more HR2 per bottle of shampoo than we do. Therefore, we do not need to consider replacing the HR2 in our shampoo with a more expensive alternative."*
>
> *Discuss how well reasoned you find this argument. In your discussion be sure to analyze the line of reasoning and the use of evidence in the argument. For example, you may need to consider what questionable Assumptions underlie the thinking and what alternative explanations or counter examples might weaken the conclusion. You can also discuss what sort of evidence would strengthen or refute the argument, what changes in the argument would make it more logically sound, and what, if anything, would help you better evaluate its conclusion.*

Strategies

A good place to start your analysis is by creating a statement that reveals the main idea of the argument. Although the writer is creating an argument, he may ultimately be stating a position, making a recommendation, or making a prediction. It may be helpful for you to determine which of these formats is most evident in the argument.

Recommendation

The company should continue to use HR2 in their shampoo because there have been no customer complaints and other shampoo companies also use the compound.

The directions for crafting your response include suggesting that you identify any questionable assumptions that may underlie or support the writer's conclusion. The assumptions may be stated or implied.

Claims and/or Assumptions

a) The lack of complaints indicates customers are not experiencing hair loss

b) The term "prolonged use" refers to a time period of one year or less

c) The size of the bottles of shampoo sold by competitors is the same as that of this company

d) There are no chemical compounds that, if combined with HR2, mitigate the risk of hair loss.

The author of the argument may have omitted some information to make his position appear stronger. What information would help you decide if the argument has validity or what should the writer's audience know in order to make an informed decision?

Additional information needed to analyze the argument

a) What length of time is indicated by "prolonged use."

b) The results of the study that indicated a risk of hair loss.

c) The size of bottles of shampoo marketed by competitors that use more HR2

d) The size of this company's bottles of shampoo

e) The method by which customer complaints are received and tabulated

Sample Essay

In this internal memorandum the CEO of this shampoo company advises that the company will continue to use the chemical HR2 in its shampoos, despite some recent information that it may lead to hair loss. He asserts his position based on the limits of the study that indicated the hair loss problem, by citing the lack of customer complaints, and by noting that some of the company's competitors actually use more HR2 in their shampoos. The CEO has made several assumptions and omitted key information, and, therefore, his recommendation is not sound.

The CEO feels his position is buoyed by the limits of the study, which included only 500 participants. While it may be the case that the survey population was not generally representative of the average user of the company's shampoo, more information is required in order to make this point. The CEO should include demographic information about the average user of the shampoo, and compare that information to the study sample. If, for example, the shampoo is most popular with teenage boys living in the northeast, and the study was conducted exclusively with teenage boys in the northeast, then the results would be directly relevant to the CEO's product and would demonstrate a need for more study before dismissing them. The CEO must show that the limits of the survey mean that it is not applicable to his customer base.

In addition, there is the question of what is meant by "prolonged use." The CEO does not include information about the duration of the study cited. He also notes that the company has not received any complaints about the shampoo in the last year, or twelve months. If the hair-loss caused by HR2 tends to occur after 18 months, it could be that the CEO's current confidence is misplaced, and that, in six months, the company will be buried with complaints from balding customers. Unless the CEO provides information about the duration of the study and the amount of time required to show the noted hair loss, the lack of complaints in the past year is irrelevant.

Further, the CEO does not explain the process by which customers may submit complaints. Perhaps customers who wish to leave feedback are presented with a standardized form on which to rate their satisfaction and that form does not provide opportunity for individual feedback, specifically that the customer is suffering hair loss. It may also be that customer complaints are routed through several different departments and handled automatically with coupons for free products or other incentives, and there is no means by which the CEO is made aware of complaints.

The CEO further argues that some of their competitors use more HR2 per bottle of shampoo than his company, offering that fact as more evidence that there is no danger for customers and that they should continue to use HR2. However, the CEO does not offer information about the relative sizes of the bottles of shampoo sold by either company. For example, if the CEO's company sells six ounce bottles of shampoo which contain 4 ounces of HR2 and their competitors typically sell 36 ounce bottles of shampoo containing 4.5 ounces of HR2, then although the competitors use more of the chemical, the concentration is much lower and customers are exposed to less of the chemical, making it less likely that they will experience the adverse effects with prolonged use.

The CEO is understandably concerned with the cost of replacing HR2 with a more expensive additive. However, he has not shown that the chemical is safe for customer use and has not provided the evidence necessary to prove that customers using their shampoo will not experience adverse effects.

Argument Task 11

The following appeared as part of an annual report sent to stockholders by Olympic Foods, a processor of frozen foods:

"Over time, the costs of processing go down because as organizations learn how to do things better, they become more efficient. In color film processing, for example, the cost of a 3-by-5-inch print fell from 50 cents for five-day service in 1970 to 20 cents for one-day service in 1984. The same principle applies to the processing of food. And since Olympic Foods will soon celebrate its 25th birthday, we can expect that our long experience will enable us to minimize costs and thus maximize profits."

Discuss how well reasoned you find this argument. In your discussion be sure to analyze the line of reasoning and the use of evidence in the argument. For example, you may need to consider what questionable Assumptions underlie the thinking and what alternative explanations or counter examples might weaken the conclusion. You can also discuss what sort of evidence would strengthen or refute the argument, what changes in the argument would make it more logically sound, and what, if anything, would help you better evaluate its conclusion.

Strategies

A good place to start your analysis is by creating a statement that reveals the main idea of the argument. Although the writer is creating an argument, he may ultimately be stating a position, making a recommendation, or making a prediction. It may be helpful for you to determine which of these formats is most evident in the argument.

Argument

Companies that have been in business for a long time are able to use their experience to reduce processing costs, and this applies to Olympic Foods.

Olympic Foods' long experience will enable them to minimize costs and maximize profits.

The directions for crafting your response include suggesting that you identify any questionable Assumptions that may underlie or support the writer's conclusion. The Assumptions may be stated or implied.

Claims and/or Assumptions

   a)   Cost of processing declines as more efficient methods are employed

   b)   Reduction in cost of processing a 3x5 print is a result of greater efficiency

   c)   Reduction in cost of processing film will translate into reduction in cost of food processing

   d)   25 years of experience should make Olympic Foods more profitable

   e)   Longevity creates efficiency

To help you create your analysis of the argument, list alternative explanations for the claims made in the

argument. What else may explain the events listed? What claims might someone on the opposite side of the argument make?

Alternative explanations/counter examples

a) Materials used for processing prints may be less expensive than they were in 1970

b) The volume of prints may have reduced the cost of individual prints

c) Processing film is very different from processing frozen food; efficiency in one industry may not translate to another industry

d) Longevity does not necessarily lead to efficiency. Some very old companies take great pride in doing things the old-fashioned way; some new companies are efficient from the outset

The author of the argument may have omitted some information to make his position appear stronger. What information would help you decide if the argument has validity or what should the writer's audience know in order to make an informed decision?

Additional information needed to better evaluate the argument

a) Have other costs of processing risen, thereby offsetting the savings in processing?

b) Have increased costs in labor, insurance, etc. forced companies to use less expensive materials in processing?

c) The motive for the report- to satisfy stockholders?

d) Specificity about ways to increase profitability

e) The company's financial health in previous years

After completing these steps, you should have enough material to write your analysis. Remember that you are not creating a position of your own; you are evaluating the strengths and weaknesses of the existing argument. You do not have to include all of the points that you have created in your prewriting. In fact, during the process of drafting your analysis, other ideas may come to mind, and, if they strengthen your analysis, you should include them.

Sample Essay

It might seem logical that a company, over time, would use its experience to reduce expenses by streamlining its processing operations. The author of this argument has used the example of photo processing to justify his belief that the same result will accrue in the processing of frozen foods. Not only is it a stretch to compare two such disparate industries, it is unwise to do so without more information or considering alternative explanations for the apparently successful reduction in operating costs in the photo processing industry.

Since this argument is part of a report sent to stockholders, the likely purpose of the argument is to reassure stockholders about their choice of Olympic Foods as an investment. Stockholders expect companies in which they have invested to pay dividends on their stocks every quarter. It may be that Olympic Foods has failed to show a profit, and the stockholders have some concerns about the future of the company. To boost the confidence of stockholders, the company has used some non specific language to paint a rosy picture of the future. The phrase "over time" in the first sentence fails to reveal how much time it takes a specific business to reduce the cost of processing through greater efficiency. In the final sentence, the report includes the phrase "we can expect" to proclaim the likelihood of maximizing profits. Expectations are not enough to create success. In order to convince stockholders, the company should present a detailed timeline of actions it plans to take to minimize costs and maximize profits.

Using the photo processing industry to bolster its argument is suspect at best and spurious at the worst. It is, in effect, an attempt to divert the attention of the stockholders from what may actually be happening at Olympic Foods. The company appears to have used real evidence from the photo processing industry to demonstrate how the cost of processing can be reduced, but there is missing information. Over the fourteen-year period cited in the report, a number of events may have occurred to reduce the cost of processing photos. An increase in volume, alone, may account for the reduced prices. Today, one can even go to Wal-Mart or a drug store and process his or her own prints for pennies apiece.

The cost of doing business for Olympic Foods involves more than just processing expenses. Increased efficiency in that area of the industry may be offset by rising utility costs, higher wages, pricey packaging, or greater prices for raw materials. Focusing on the cost of processing may be aimed at distracting the stockholders from other aspects of the business that could have a negative impact on profitability. In order to protect their investment, the stockholders should demand to see a complete accounting of expenses and earnings.

Argument Task 12

> *The following appeared in a memorandum issued by a large city's council on the arts:*
>
> *"In a recent citywide poll, 15 percent more residents said that they watch television programs about the visual arts than was the case in a poll conducted five years ago. During these past five years, the number of people visiting our city's art museums has increased by a similar percentage. Since the corporate funding that supports public television, where most of the visual arts programs appear, is now being threatened with severe cuts, we can expect that attendance at our city's art museums will also start to decrease. Thus some of the city's funds for supporting the arts should be reallocated to public television."*
>
> *Discuss how well reasoned you find this argument. In your discussion be sure to analyze the line of reasoning and the use of evidence in the argument. For example, you may need to consider what questionable Assumptions unlike the thinking and what alternative explanations or counter examples might weaken the conclusion. You can also discuss what sort of evidence would strengthen or refute the argument, what changes in the argument would make it more logically sound, and what, if anything, would help you better evaluate its conclusion.*

Strategies

A good place to start your analysis is by creating a statement that reveals the main idea of the argument. Although the writer is creating an argument, he may ultimately be stating a position, making a recommendation, or making a prediction. It may be helpful for you to determine which of these formats is most evident in the argument.

Recommendation

Some of the city's funds for supporting the arts should be reallocated to public television.

The directions for crafting your response include suggesting that you identify any questionable Assumptions that may underlie or support the writer's conclusion. The Assumptions may be stated or implied.

Claims and/or Assumptions

a) The same people were surveyed both times

b) Citizens are watching TV programs about the visual arts instead of other types of programs

c) The same programs are being offered that were available 5 years ago

d) There is a correlation between increased visits to city's art museum and increased viewing of programs about visual arts

e) People are watching programs about visual arts only on public television

f) Reduced funding of public television will lead to fewer visits to the local museum

g) 15% more is a significant number

h)   The same number of television channels exists as did five years ago

To help you create your analysis of the argument, list alternative explanations for the claims made in the argument. What else may explain the events listed? What claims might someone on the opposite side of the argument make?

Alternative explanations or counter claims

a)   A different segment of the population may have been polled in the second survey

b)   It may be that more networks are offering programs about the visual arts, thus increasing the likelihood of viewers being able to see one

c)   The art museum may have had more interesting or popular exhibits during the period in question

d)   If citizens cannot see programs about the visual arts on TV they may make more visits to the museum

e)   Fewer television channels -or more- are available than were five years ago

The author of the argument may have omitted some information to make his position appear stronger. What information would help you decide if the argument has validity or what should the writer's audience know in order to make an informed decision?

Additional information needed

a)   Which influenced the other? Did people visit the museum after watching TV shows, or did they watch more shows after visiting the museum?

b)   Has the admission price at the museum declined, making it more affordable for more people?

c)   Actual numbers instead of percentages

d)   What else may have influenced the increases, e.g., special events, weather, economic conditions

Sample Essay

This argument uses a cause-and-effect line of reasoning to support the recommendation that the city move some of its funds that support the arts to help fund public television. The cause is a 15 percent increase in the number of visual arts programs viewed by participants in a survey. The effect is a similar increase in the number of people visiting the city's art museums. Because public television funding is being threatened, the city's council on the arts fears that museum attendance will decline and offers this rationale to support the recommendation. Before reallocating funds, the city leaders should carefully analyze the argument offered by the arts council and seek additional information.

Percentages can be misleading. A 15 percent increase is significant if the original number is relatively high. If the survey conducted five years ago revealed that 40 respondents watched programs about the visual arts, a 15 percent increase would mean that now 46 respondents watch those programs. Six additional viewers over a five-year span are not enough to justify changing decisions about funding. The argument claims that a similar increase in visits to the city's arts museums occurred over the same period of time. Decision makers cannot determine if the actual increase is greater or less than 15 percent, but, again, the actual numbers would be more telling.

The council on the arts may want to know if there are other reasons for increased attendance at the museums. Has the admission price been reduced, making it more affordable for families to visit the arts museums? Perhaps the museums have installed more attractive exhibits that have a broader appeal. They may also have conducted a strong marketing campaign to encourage more citizens to visit. The council should also take a closer look at television viewership. Why are more people watching television shows about the visual arts? There may be fewer television stations serving this market than there were five years ago. With fewer programming choices, more people are tuning in to public television, where most of these shows are aired.

Another point of inspection is the actual timing of the increase in both television viewing and museum visits. If the increases occurred concurrently and evenly over the five year period, then considering those numbers is a valid point. If, however, one or both of those increases occurred in the first year of the five-year span, the numbers are misleading and manipulative. The same is true if the increases occurred in the last year of the span. A one-year increase is an anomaly, not a trend.

Finally, the city leaders must determine if there actually is a cause-and-effect relationship, and, if one exists, which event influenced the other. Did citizens watch more television shows after visiting the city's art museums, or did they visit the art museums after watching the television shows? Based on the paucity of information in the memorandum, the leadership cannot eliminate the possibility that the events are simply coincidental and cannot shift funding without a more detailed rationale.

Argument Task 13

The following appeared in a report presented for discussion at a meeting of the directors of a company that manufactures parts for heavy machinery:

"The falling revenues that the company is experiencing coincide with delays in manufacturing. These delays, in turn, are due in large part to poor planning in purchasing metals. Consider further that the manager of the department that handles purchasing of raw materials has an excellent background in general business, psychology, and sociology, but knows little about the properties of metals. The company should, therefore, move the purchasing manager to the sales department and bring in a scientist from the research division to be manager of the purchasing department."

Discuss how well reasoned you find this argument. In your discussion be sure to analyze the line of reasoning and the use of evidence in the argument. For example, you may need to consider what questionable Assumptions unlike the thinking and what alternative explanations or counter examples might weaken the conclusion. You can also discuss what sort of evidence would strengthen or refute the argument, what changes in the argument would make it more logically sound, and what, if anything, would help you better evaluate its conclusion.

Strategies

A good place to start your analysis is by creating a statement that reveals the main idea of the argument. Although the writer is creating an argument, he may ultimately be stating a position, making a recommendation, or making a prediction. It may be helpful for you to determine which of these formats is most evident in the argument.

Recommendation

The company should move the purchasing manager to the sales department and bring in a scientist from the research division to be manager of the purchasing department.

The directions for crafting your response include suggesting that you identify any questionable Assumptions that may underlie or support the writer's conclusion. The Assumptions may be stated or implied.

Claims and/or Assumptions

a) A scientist would be a better purchasing manager than someone with a business background

b) Delays in manufacturing are the cause of falling revenues

c) Knowledge of the properties of metals is necessary to be an effective purchasing manager

d) Delays in manufacturing are have occurred because the purchasing manager has not planned well

e) The purchasing manager will be more effective in the sales department

f) An excellent background in general business, psychology, and sociology make one perform better in sales than in purchasing

To help you create your analysis of the argument, list alternative explanations for the claims made in the argument. What else may explain the events listed? What claims might someone on the opposite side of the argument make?

Alternative explanations and counter examples

a) Falling revenues may be a result of reduced demand

b) Falling revenues can result from failing to compensate for higher costs of raw materials

c) There may be more competition from other manufacturers

d) Knowledge of the properties of metal is important in the design and manufacturing process

e) Many companies train their department heads, disregarding what they may have taken for courses in college

The author of the argument may have omitted some information to make his position appear stronger. What information would help you decide if the argument has validity or what should the writer's audience know in order to make an informed decision?

Additional information needed to analyze the argument

a) How long the purchasing manager has been in that position and his track record

b) For how long revenues have been declining

c) The type of heavy machinery the company manufactures

d) Conditions in the market that have affected sales

e) The availability of metals needed for manufacturing

f) How much training the company provides for its department managers

Sample Essay

The author of this report has listed a number of causes that have contributed to the effect of falling revenues. The recommendation to shift personnel within the company appears to be an attempt to reverse the decline. Before the directors accept this recommendation, they should examine the series of events delineated in the report to determine if they are, indeed, part of a domino effect leading to a decline in revenues, or if they are simply coincidental, occurring at the same time but having nothing to do with each other.

Falling revenues is cause for concern, and the company leadership should determine the cause as quickly as possible. Because the report identifies the purchasing manner as largely responsible for the downturn, the directors should look closely at his employment record with the company. If he has been with the company in this position for several years and has a heretofore unblemished record, it may be premature to reassign both him and a scientist from the research division. On the other hand, the purchasing manager may have been recently promoted to or hired for this position and, in a short period of time, has made several costly blunders. In this case, it may be in the company's best interest to reassign him or, at the very least, provide additional training during a probationary period. Before moving a scientist into the purchasing department, the directors should examine his or her qualifications in that area. The scientist selected to replace the purchasing manager may be insulted, or may feel that his or her specialized education will be underutilized in purchasing. The current purchasing manager, also, may be disappointed or unqualified for a position in sales. If he or she is ineffectual in purchasing, the directors might consider releasing him/her from the company altogether.

Although it may appear that poor planning on the part of the purchasing manager has led to a short supply of manufacturing materials, factors beyond his control may be in play. Mines producing some metals may be depleted, and new sources have yet to be discovered. Transportation of raw materials from some areas may be affected by seasonal challenges like floods or blizzards. Miners could be on strike, or an accident could have occurred at a mine.

Market conditions must always be examined when a company's revenues decline. Demand for the heavy machinery produced by the company may have disappeared. For example, the current drought in the central portion of the United States has resulted in serious crop failures. Without the income generated from harvesting and selling agricultural staples, those growers cannot buy new machinery. Because this drought is widespread, thousands of growers must postpone purchases. This cannot help but affect manufacturers. The purchasing manager, in fact, may have made a deliberate decision to order less material based on information received from the sales department. Regardless of the industry that this company produces machinery for, conditions beyond the control of the purchasing manager may affect revenues.

Finally, it would be important for the directors to consider previous years' revenues. If this current decline is part of a pattern, the directors must consider more widespread changes than shifting around some personnel. The company may need to shift its focus, seek new sources of raw materials, scout the competition, or make changes in personnel in an effort to increase revenues.

Argument Task 14

The following appeared in the health section of a magazine on trends and lifestyles:

"People who use the artificial sweetener aspartame are better off consuming sugar, since aspartame can actually contribute to weight gain rather than weight loss. For example, high levels of aspartame have been shown to trigger a craving for food by depleting the brain of a chemical that registers satiety, or the sense of being full. Furthermore, studies suggest that sugars, if consumed after at least 45 minutes of continuous exercise, actually enhance the body's ability to burn fat. Consequently, those who drink aspartame-sweetened juices after exercise will also lose this calorie-burning benefit. Thus it appears that people consuming aspartame rather than sugar are unlikely to achieve their dietary goals."

Discuss how well reasoned you find this argument. In your discussion be sure to analyze the line of reasoning and the use of evidence in the argument. For example, you may need to consider what questionable Assumptions unlike the thinking and what alternative explanations or counter examples might weaken the conclusion. You can also discuss what sort of evidence would strengthen or refute the argument, what changes in the argument would make it more logically sound, and what, if anything, would help you better evaluate its conclusion.

Strategies

A good place to start your analysis is by creating a statement that reveals the main idea of the argument. Although the writer is creating an argument, he may ultimately be stating a position, making a recommendation, or making a prediction. It may be helpful for you to determine which of these formats is most evident in the argument.

Prediction

People who consume aspartame rather than sugar are not likely to achieve their dietary goals.

The directions for crafting your response include suggesting that you identify any questionable Assumptions that may underlie or support the writer's conclusion. The Assumptions may be stated or implied.

Claims and/or Assumptions

   a) Consumption of aspartame leads to weight gain

   b) High levels of aspartame trigger a craving for food by depleting the chemical that registers satiety in the brain

   c) Consumption of sugar does not contribute to weight gain

   d) Sugar contributes to the body's ability to burn fat

   e) The author is citing studies done with human subjects

To help you create your analysis of the argument, list alternative explanations for the claims made in the

argument. What else may explain the events listed? What claims might someone on the opposite side of the argument make?

Alternative explanations/counter examples

a) Aspartame alone is not likely to cause weight gain

b) A number of factors contribute to weight loss/gain

c) The benefits of consuming sugar occur only after strenuous exercise

d) Strenuous exercise alone is sufficient to cause the body to burn fat

e) Dietary goals may be to control diabetes

f) The author is using findings from studies done on animals

The author of the argument may have omitted some information to make his position appear stronger. What information would help you decide if the argument has validity or what should the writer's audience know in order to make an informed decision?

Additional information needed to better evaluate the argument

a) Were the studies conducted on humans?

b) How much aspartame must be consumed to reach the levels cited in the argument?

c) Who conducted the study?

d) How much is fat-burning ability enhanced by sugar consumption after exercise?

e) The intended audience for the magazine

f) How much space in the magazine is devoted to health topics?

g) The dietary goals of people who consume aspartame

Sample Essay

Any time that new claims about a food product appear, consumers should read and listen with a fair amount of skepticism. Over the years, we have been warned about the negative consequences of eating bacon, eggs, white bread and pasta, or drinking coffee, fruit juices, or alcohol. Nutrition gurus have promoted the benefits of low-carbohydrates consumption, the grapefruit diet, or the Paleo diet. Scientists have proclaimed the benefits of photochemical and getting sufficient Vitamin D. Dieters spend millions of dollars each year on food sent to their homes from Jenny Craig or Nutrisystem or to attend meetings conducted by Weight Watchers. Everyone, it seems, is seeking that magic bullet for losing weight. Now, this article touts the benefits of sugar over aspartame in meeting one's dietary goals.

Dietary goals may be different for everyone and can change over time. An individual's dietary goal may not necessarily be to lose weight. People with any type of diabetes must control their carbohydrate and sugar consumption. Any benefits that are gained from post-exercise sugar consumption would be negated in the diabetic's body. As people age, their dietary goals may change as well. Young people may want to emulate models whose ultra-thin bodies appear in fashion magazines, while older people may simply want to sustain a sensible weight for their age and activity level.

When a study of consumables uses the phrase "high levels", the reader should always ask at least two important questions. First, what amount constitutes a high level? How much of a food or beverage sweetened with aspartame would an individual have to ingest to reach those high levels? Those levels are apt to be determined in a laboratory setting and have no practical equivalent in the real world. For example, if one would have to drink 3 liters of aspartame-sweetened juice to achieve those levels, it is unlikely that many people will be in danger of the depleting the brain chemical that signals satiety. There is no information in the argument that tells how quickly the body metabolizes aspartame. If it accumulates and remains in one's system for a long period of time, the cited reaction might be a reality. Along with questioning the levels, consumers should ask who the test subjects were. We're the tests conducted on humans, or did the scientists use lab mice or other animals? Results obtained in a lab using animals may not always apply to humans.

Readers should seek more studies that have been done on the effect that the feeling of satiety has on diet. If everyone stopped eating when they feel full, there would be no obesity problem. Whether aspartame consumption or some other dietary component interferes with that feeling needs more substantiation. Aspartame, which is an artificial sweetener, may have additional or greater dangers than those cited in this argument, but encouraging sugar consumption may also have its downsides. At the end of the day, does consuming sugar after exercise burn enough calories to make it worthwhile, or is the exercise, itself, sufficient?

Argument Task 15

> *The following appeared in the editorial section of a local newspaper:*
>
> *"This past winter, 200 students from Waymarsh State College traveled to the state capitol building to protest against proposed cuts in funding for various state college programs. The other 12,000 Waymarsh students evidently weren't so concerned about their education: they either stayed on campus or left for winter break. Since the group who did not protest is far more numerous, it is more representative of the state's college students than are the protesters. Therefore the state legislature need not heed the appeals of the protesting students."*
>
> *Discuss how well reasoned you find this argument. In your discussion be sure to analyze the line of reasoning and the use of evidence in the argument. For example, you may need to consider what questionable Assumptions unlike the thinking and what alternative explanations or counter examples might weaken the conclusion. You can also discuss what sort of evidence would strengthen or refute the argument, what changes in the argument would make it more logically sound, and what, if anything, would help you better evaluate its conclusion.*

Strategies

A good place to start your analysis is by creating a statement that reveals the main idea of the argument. Although the writer is creating an argument, he may ultimately be stating a position, making a recommendation, or making a prediction. It may be helpful for you to determine which of these formats is most evident in the argument.

Argument

Because only 200 of the 12000 students who attend Waymarsh College protested proposed cuts in various state college programs, legislators can ignore the appeals of the protesters.

The directions for crafting your response include suggesting that you identify any questionable Assumptions that may underlie or support the writer's conclusion. The Assumptions may be stated or implied.

Claims and/or Assumptions

   a) The 12,000 students who did not go to the state Capitol building are not concerned about their
       education

   b) Only the 200 students who protested the cuts care about their education

To help you create your analysis of the argument, list alternative explanations for the claims made in the argument. What else may explain the events listed? What claims might someone on the opposite side of the argument make?

Alternative explanations or counter claims

   a) The 200 may have been selected to represent all students at Waymarsh

    b)   The 200 who went to the Capitol building may have those directly affected by the proposed funding cuts

    c)   The students who remained on campus may have had academic obligations

The author of the argument may have omitted some information to make his position appear stronger. What information would help you decide if the argument has validity or what should the writer's audience know in order to make an informed decision?

Additional information needed to better evaluate the argument

    a)   If the 200 protesters have a vested interest in the proposed cuts

    b)   If the 200 were selected by the student body or university officials to represent the entire school

Sample Essay

An editorial, by its nature, expresses an opinion. It is the author's opinion that the students who did not make the trip to the Capitol building see no cause for concern with proposed funding cuts for Waymarsh State College. His recommendation is for the state legislature to ignore the pleas of the protesters. It would have been highly impractical for all 12,000 students to make the journey. History is replete with example of the few speaking for the many, much as the legislature itself does.

Americans take for granted that the original signers of the Declaration of Independence were speaking for the majority of the residents of the new country. Imagine if everyone living in the thirteen colonies had made the trip to Philadelphia or had needed to in order for Great Britain to take the desire for independence seriously. King George III may very well have said, "Since only 56 individuals signed this document, we can ignore their plea for independence." We know that he took it seriously enough to engage in a war that would prevent the separation of the colonies from the Motherland.

Just as the drafters and signers of the Declaration of Independence represented the desires of everyone living in the colonies, the 200 students from Waymarsh State College may represent the concerns of a majority of the 12,000 who didn't attend the protest. These protesters may have been selected by the larger student body to carry their sentiments to the legislative body. Based on this author's argument, one would be justified in ignoring the decision of the legislature since the members of that body are a very small sample of the state's entire population. The author also implies that the 12,000 who stayed behind did so for frivolous reasons. He claims that they either stayed on campus or left for winter break but fails to reveal how many students did each of those. Those who stayed on campus may have elected to take courses during a winter term, and that obligation prevented them from attending the protest.

An additional missing piece of information is the distribution of Waymarsh students in the programs offered on the campus. The 200 protesters may be enrolled in a program of study more threatened by the proposed cuts than other programs. Some of them may have invested more than two years and many thousands of dollars in their programs and would be forced to change majors or transfer to another university. In a time when colleges and universities are challenged to fill their classrooms, the potential loss of 200 students could be significant. The legislature should consider the benefit of either making the cuts or losing enrollment.

The author of the argument does not identify the types of programs that are on the chopping block. They may not be academic programs, but, instead, services for students, such as health care or career placement. The reader also doesn't know if the university may be able to offer those programs online, an option that many schools are adopting today to both save money and lengthen their reach into the pool of potential students.

In the final analysis, readers of this editorial shouldn't jump on the bandwagon until they have more information. They are sure to understand that once something is gone, it doesn't come back. The legislatures must carefully decide if the savings are worth the ultimate cost of cutting programs at Waymarsh State College.

Argument Task 16

> *The following appeared as part of a promotional campaign to sell advertising space in the Daily Gazette to grocery stores in the Marston area:*
>
> *"Advertising the reduced price of selected grocery items in the Daily Gazette will help you increase your sales. Consider the results of a study conducted last month. Thirty sale items from a store in downtown Marston were advertised in The Gazette for four days. Each time one or more of the 30 items was purchased; clerks asked whether the shopper had read the ad Two-thirds of the 200 shoppers asked answered in the affirmative. Furthermore, more than half the customers who answered in the affirmative spent over $100 at the store."*
>
> *Discuss how well reasoned you find this argument. In your discussion be sure to analyze the line of reasoning and the use of evidence in the argument. For example, you may need to consider what questionable Assumptions unlike the thinking and what alternative explanations or counter examples might weaken the conclusion. You can also discuss what sort of evidence would strengthen or refute the argument, what changes in the argument would make it more logically sound, and what, if anything, would help you better evaluate its conclusion.*

Strategies

A good place to start your analysis is by creating a statement that reveals the main idea of the argument. Although the writer is creating an argument, he may ultimately be stating a position, making a recommendation, or making a prediction. It may be helpful for you to determine which of these formats is most evident in the argument.

Prediction

Advertising the reduced price of selected grocery items in the Daily Gazette will increase your sales.

The directions for crafting your response include suggesting that you identify any questionable Assumptions that may underlie or support the writer's conclusion. The Assumptions may be stated or implied.

Claims and/or Assumptions

   a)   Advertising in the Daily Gazette increased sales

   b)   Customers spent more than they usually do

   c)   Customers bought more items than they normally do

   d)   The store that advertised is a grocery store

   e)   An increase in sales leads to an increase in profits

   f)   Most of the shoppers had read the ad and purchased the items

To help you create your analysis of the argument, list alternative explanations for the claims made in the argument. What else may explain the events listed? What claims might someone on the opposite side of the argument make?

Alternative explanations and/or counter claims

a) The advertised items may have been big-ticket items, so a customer would not have to buy many to spend $100

b) It may have been during the days prior to Thanksgiving, when people buy more food than they usually do

c) 200 customers may have been a small part of the total customer count

The author of the argument may have omitted some information to make his position appear stronger. What information would help you decide if the argument has validity or what should the writer's audience know in order to make an informed decision?

Additional information needed to better evaluate the argument

a) The total number of shoppers over the four-day period

b) How sales of the 30 items compared to sales before advertising

c) How much of a reduction in prices

d) Was the store cited a grocery store?

e) During which month the sale took place

Sample Essay

Effective advertising is important to the success of virtually every business. What to advertise, when to advertise, and which medium to use are choices that can determine the return on the dollars spent. Because newspapers rely on advertising revenues for their existence, they must make it sound advantageous to use them to spread the word about a company's product or service. They will do what they must to make it attractive to the business owner, but that business person would be advised to ask pertinent questions and seek enough additional information to make a wise decision.

According to the author do this argument, advertising reduced prices in the Daily Gazette will increase sales. While increasing sales is the goal of any business, doing so at reduced prices can have a detrimental effect on profits. For example, if a store sells 100 units of Item A at the full price of $10 per unit, the store has generated $1000 in sales. At the sale price of $9, the same store sells 150 of the item, generating $1350 in sales. On the surface, the store has an extra $350. If the item cost the business $8, the profit on 100 items at full price is $200, but on 150 items at the sale price, the profit is only $150. The store has sold an additional 50 items but has $50 fewer with which to pay the bills.

Citing a study conducted the previous month, the promotional campaign states that two-thirds of the 200 customers who bought advertised items had seen the ad. This number would carry more or less weight depending on the actual customer count for the period in question. If there were a total of 200 customers during the four days that the ad circulated, then two thirds, or roughly 132, is significant. However, if the total customer count were 1000, then 132 is not as meaningful. The campaign goes on to reveal that half of the 132 customers, or 61, spent more than $100. Again, the total customer count determines the strength of the claim.

Equally important for the grocery business in particular is the month during which the study was conducted. If the ad ran during the four days prior to Thanksgiving, for example, the figures become meaningless for any other period. Thanksgiving is the biggest food holiday of the year, and virtually every customer will spend more than usual. If the ad ran during an otherwise slow period for grocery sales and produced higher sales, The Daily Gazette has a stronger argument for purchasing ad space.

A final assumption that must be verified or denied is that the store in Marston whose sales are cited in the argument is, indeed, a grocery store. The argument does not specify which type of store in downtown Marston advertised for four days last month. Using the success of one retail segment to build an argument for sales of advertising to another retail segment is spurious. The client should ask to see how other grocery stores have fared with the Daily Gazette's advertising. Additionally, the store cited in the argument may face stiff competition in the Marston area and is forced to pursue aggressive marketing strategies. On the other hand, there may be only one grocery store. With no competition, the grocer may elect to spend his advertising budget in a different manner.

After consideration of the claims made in the argument and scrutiny of the market and his own needs, the grocer can make a more informed decision about the efficacy of purchasing advertising space in the Daily Gazette.

Argument Task 17

> *The following appeared as a part of an advertisement for Adams, who is seeking reelection as governor:*
>
> *"Reelect Adams and you will be voting for proven leadership in improving the state's economy. Over the past year alone, 70 percent of the state's workers have had increases in their wages, 5,000 new jobs have been created, and six corporations have located their headquarters here. Most of the respondents in a recent poll said they believed that the economy is likely to continue to improve if Adams is reelected. Adams's opponent, Zebulon, would lead our state in the wrong direction, because Zebulon disagrees with many of Adams's economic policies."*
>
> *Discuss how well reasoned you find this argument. In your discussion be sure to analyze the line of reasoning and the use of evidence in the argument. For example, you may need to consider what questionable Assumptions unlike the thinking and what alternative explanations or counter examples might weaken the conclusion. You can also discuss what sort of evidence would strengthen or refute the argument, what changes in the argument would make it more logically sound, and what, if anything, would help you better evaluate its conclusion.*

Strategies

A good place to start your analysis is by creating a statement that reveals the main idea of the argument. Although the writer is creating an argument, he may ultimately be stating a position, making a recommendation, or making a prediction. It may be helpful for you to determine which of these formats is most evident in the argument.

Argument

Electing Adams will lead to continued economic progress.

The directions for crafting your response include suggesting that you identify any questionable Assumptions that may underlie or support the writer's conclusion. The Assumptions may be stated or implied.

Claims and/or Assumptions

a) Adams' economic policies are the reason that workers saw an increase in wages

b) Adams' economic policies caused six corporations to move to the state

c) Adams' economic policies helped to create 5000 new jobs

d) Zebulon disagrees with the economic policies that created growth in the state

e) Respondents in a recent poll believe that the economy will continue to improve if Adams is reelected

To help you create your analysis of the argument, list alternative explanations for the claims made in the argument. What else may explain the events listed? What claims might someone on the opposite side of the argument make?

Alternative explanations and counter claims

a) Workers may have received a scheduled raise

b) The companies that moved to the state did not replace the number of companies that left the state in the same period of time

c) The jobs created did not equal or surpass the number of jobs lost during the same time period

d) Zebulon may have plans of his own for economic growth in the state

The author of the argument may have omitted some information to make his position appear stronger. What information would help you decide if the argument has validity or what should the writer's audience know in order to make an informed decision?

Additional information needed to better evaluate the argument

a) How many workers received a raise in preceding years?

b) How many jobs were created or lost in preceding years

c) How many companies left the state or relocated to the state in preceding years

d) Whether or not Adams' administration offered financial incentives to companies moving to the state

e) Zebulon's economic policy

f) The condition of the state's economy when Adams took office

Sample Essay

The economy is always a hot-button issue in an election year. Campaign managers attempt to make their own candidate's record look stellar while pointing out the deficiencies in the opponents' records. Voters must always keep in mind that the purpose of any advertisement is to sell a product or service. In the case of a political ad, it is to sell a candidate by pointing out the advantages of electing him or her.

This particular advertisement makes it appear that Adams is responsible for 70 percent of the State's workers receiving an increase in pay. While that may be true, the voters need more information before accepting the veracity of the statement. Does this increase put the workers on a par with workers in the same industries in other states, or are wages in Adams' state still below the national average? Increased pay does not mean much unless it effectively raises the workers' standard of living. If an Adams policy is responsible for the increase, did he offer tax breaks or other incentives to business to make it possible for them to pay their workers more? Additionally, if there were tax breaks, how will that affect state funding for infrastructure or education? It is also possible that the pay increases were part of multi-year contracts negotiated by labor unions. Teachers, for example, generally work under contracts that are negotiated every three or four years, and their salary increase could be a significant contributor to the 70 percent.

Another example of Adams' efficacy is the move to the state by the headquarters of six companies. On the surface, this claim sounds like a reason to vote for Adams. However, some companies house their headquarters in a different state or country from where the work actually takes place. If these companies have moved their manufacturing plants to the state, they may have created thousands of jobs; if not, those companies are merely renting or buying office space. Wal-Mart, for example, has its headquarters in Benton, Arkansas, but the jobs generated by the Wal-Mart Corporation exist in states around the country where their stores are built or their merchandise is manufactured. New headquarters in the state may not translate to job creation. The voter also doesn't know if the same number or more companies have left the state during the same time period.

The next feather in Adams' cap is the creation of 5000 new jobs during his tenure. States are always seeking job creation, and if, in fact, Adams' state has had a net gain of 5000 jobs that is quite a coup. What is not revealed is whether jobs have left the state as well. It would be helpful to know what kinds of jobs comprise the 5000. If most of them are in the service industry, they are not high-paying jobs and are unlikely to include benefits. On the other hand, if they are manufacturing jobs, they may generate high incomes and provide health and retirement benefits.

According to the poll cited in the advertisement, the residents of the state believe that Adams is responsible for economic prosperity and that the trend will continue if he is reelected. The ad further states that Adams' opponent, Zebulon, would lead the state in a different direction because he disagrees with many of Adams' economic policies. The voter doesn't know which policies those are and should not base his decision in the voting booth based on a general statement like this. As in any election, voters must rely on their own willingness to research the candidates' records before choosing a leader for the next four years.

Argument Task 18

> *The following appeared in an article in a consumer-products magazine:*
>
> *"Two of today's best-selling brands of full-strength prescription medication for the relief of excess stomach acid, Acid-Ease and Pepticaid, are now available in milder nonprescription forms. Doctors have written 76 million more prescriptions for full-strength Acid-Ease than for full-strength Pepticaid. So people who need an effective but milder nonprescription medication for the relief of excess stomach acid should choose Acid-Ease."*
>
> *Discuss how well reasoned you find this argument. In your discussion be sure to analyze the line of reasoning and the use of evidence in the argument. For example, you may need to consider what questionable Assumptions unlike the thinking and what alternative explanations or counter examples might weaken the conclusion. You can also discuss what sort of evidence would strengthen or refute the argument, what changes in the argument would make it more logically sound, and what, if anything, would help you better evaluate its conclusion.*

Strategies

A good place to start your analysis is by creating a statement that reveals the main idea of the argument. Although the writer is creating an argument, he may ultimately be stating a position, making a recommendation, or making a prediction. It may be helpful for you to determine which of these formats is most evident in the argument.

Recommendation

People should choose nonprescription Acid-Ease over Pepticaid for the relief of excess stomach acid.

The directions for crafting your response include suggesting that you identify any questionable Assumptions that may underlie or support the writer's conclusion. The Assumptions may be stated or implied.

Claims and/or Assumptions

a) Both medications have been available for the same length of time

b) Acid-Ease is more effective than Pepticaid

c) Both medications are equal in all respects

To help you create your analysis of the argument, list alternative explanations for the claims made in the argument. What else may explain the events listed? What claims might someone on the opposite side of the argument make?

Alternative explanations and/or counter examples

a) Acid-Ease has been available considerably longer than Pepticaid

b) Acid-Ease may be less expensive than Pepticaid

c)   The bulk of Acid-Ease sales occurred between 10 and 5 years ago; Pepticaid has outsold Acid-Ease in the last three years

The author of the argument may have omitted some information to make his position appear stronger. What information would help you decide if the argument has validity or what should the writer's audience know in order to make an informed decision?

Additional information needed to better evaluate the argument

a)   How long each medication has been on the market

b)   The overall effectiveness of each medication

c)   If there are any side effects

d)   The price of each brand

e)   Customer reviews of each brand

Sample Essay

The purpose served by a consumer products magazine is, generally, to provide a review of the risks and benefits of buying one brand of a particular product over another brand. The review is purportedly unbiased, allowing the consumer to make his or her own choice. The magazine cited in this argument actually does recommend one product over another. Before taking the author's advice, the consumer should dig a little deeper into the reasons for the endorsement of Acid-Ease over Pepticaid.

The only concrete piece of evidence the author has provided regards the greater number of prescriptions written for Acid-Ease. 76 million more is an impressive statistic. The natural reaction on the part of the consumer is to believe that doctors must consider the product superior to its competitor, Pepticaid. One might go so far as to question how Pepticaid can even survive in the marketplace with such an enormous disparity in sales. The information needed to fairly evaluate the claim is the number of years each brand of medicine has been on the market. If Pepticaid appeared in drugstores only five years ago, while Acid-Ease has had a twenty-year run, one would expect the far greater number of sales for the latter. Consider the Ford Motor Company which began manufacturing automobiles in 1903 and Kia, which introduced its cars to the public in 1974. Undoubtedly, Ford has sold millions more vehicles than has Kia, but that is not a sufficient reason to recommend one maker over the other. Even the rate of growth is an unfair comparison. It is likely that Kia sold one million cars in a shorter period of time than did Ford. The difference in the world population between 1903 and 1974 alone would account for the more rapid growth of Kia and any other newly introduced auto manufacturers. Now, think about the two popular acid relievers. As the generation of Baby Boomers ages, more of them will be likely to need an antacid.

As with automobiles, acid relievers should be judged on their features and cost. Virtually all consumers want more bangs for their buck. If one can buy a Kia model comparable to a Ford model car but for a lower price, he or she is likely to opt for the less expensive vehicle. The author of the argument fails to reveal the benefits or cost of each medicine. If the nonprescription version of Pepticaid is as effective as the same version of Acid-Ease but costs less, consumers may ignore the recommendation of this author and decide with their pocketbooks.

Argument Task 19

The following appeared as part of an article in the travel section of a newspaper:

"Over the past decade, the restaurant industry in the country of Spiessa has experienced unprecedented growth. This surge can be expected to continue in the coming years, fueled by recent social changes: personal incomes are rising, more leisure time is available, single-person households are more common, and people have a greater interest in gourmet food, as evidenced by a proliferation of publications on the subject."

Discuss how well reasoned you find this argument. In your discussion be sure to analyze the line of reasoning and the use of evidence in the argument. For example, you may need to consider what questionable Assumptions unlike the thinking and what alternative explanations or counter examples might weaken the conclusion. You can also discuss what sort of evidence would strengthen or refute the argument, what changes in the argument would make it more logically sound, and what, if anything, would help you better evaluate its conclusion.

Strategies

A good place to start your analysis is by creating a statement that reveals the main idea of the argument. Although the writer is creating an argument, he may ultimately be stating a position, making a recommendation, or making a prediction. It may be helpful for you to determine which of these formats is most evident in the argument.

Prediction

The restaurant industry in Spiessa will continue to experience growth.

The directions for crafting your response include suggesting that you identify any questionable Assumptions that may underlie or support the writer's conclusion. The Assumptions may be stated or implied.

Claims and/or Assumptions

a) Growth in the restaurant industry has occurred consistently over the past decade

b) Social changes will cause this growth to continue

c) A proliferation in publications about gourmet food have arisen from a greater interest in gourmet food

d) Singles are more likely to eat in restaurants

e) As people's incomes rise, they are more likely to eat in restaurants

f) There are many more gourmet restaurants

To help you create your analysis of the argument, list alternative explanations for the claims made in the argument. What else may explain the events listed? What claims might someone on the opposite side of the argument make?

Alternative explanations/counter examples

a) The restaurant business barely existed prior to the past decade

b) Most of the growth occurred in one year

c) Interest in gourmet food has arisen from the proliferation of publications about gourmet food

d) Most of the growth has occurred in fast food restaurants

The author of the argument may have omitted some information to make his position appear stronger. What information would help you decide if the argument has validity or what should the writer's audience know in order to make an informed decision?

Additional information needed to better evaluate the argument

a) What types of restaurants are responsible for the growth?

b) In which years of the decade the growth occurred

c) If the cost of living has risen along with incomes

Sample Essay

The author of this article in the travel section of a newspaper predicts that the restaurant industry in Spiessa will continue to experience tremendous growth. His main reason for this belief arises from social changes that have taken place in that country. The growth may, indeed, have different causes and may be misrepresented in this article. Travelers need more information before booking a flight to Spiessa In order to sample the culinary fare.

One missing piece of information regards the decade in which the restaurant industry has experienced such growth. It would be helpful to know if the growth has been steady during the ten-year period, if the growth took place in the first year of the decade and had since stagnated, or if the growth has occurred in the last year. The statement may reflect a steady growth in places to dine, but it may be misleading, simply allowing readers to believe that is the case. If the growth has taken place in the most recent year, the restaurants may still be experiencing growing pains and not provide the dining experience visitors expect. If the bulk of the growth occurred ten years ago, the reader may wonder why it has stalled. Steady, regular growth would be a better indicator of a food business climate.

The restaurant industry encompasses more than simply places to dine. It can include manufacturers of fixtures for restaurants, suppliers of dishes and flatware, and wholesalers of food staples. If that is the case, travelers to Spiessa will not find the bounty of eateries they may be expecting. Another consideration is the types of restaurant that has appeared in Spiessa over the past decade. The article implies that they are gourmet restaurants, but they could just as well be fast-food joints. McDonalds, Subway, and others are always searching for new markets. Spiessa may have been closed to foreign companies prior to ten years ago and, since opening its borders, it has become home to chain eateries. There's no need to travel to travel to Spiessa to eat food that can be found in virtually every town in America.

Unprecedented growth means that this level of growth has never occurred before in Spiessa. If there had been no growth in the restaurant industry prior to the years ago, then any growth, however small, would be unprecedented. In fact, if there had been one restaurant in Spiessa ten years ago and now there are two, then Spiessa has experienced a 100 percent increase in the number of restaurants. Figures can be manipulated to sound better or worse than the reality of them. The list of social changes also includes some generalized figures. By now much are personal incomes rising, and is that rise restricted to a small segment of the population? More leisure time, more single-person households, and a greater interest in gourmet foods are phrases that fail to supply specific information about the socio-economic conditions in Spiessa. Without details about accommodations in Spiessa, travelers should go there at their own risk.

Argument Task 20

> *The following appeared in a memorandum from the head of a human resources department at a major automobile manufacturing company to the company's managers:*
>
> *"Studies have found that employees of not-for-profit organizations and charities are often more highly motivated than employees of for-profit corporations to perform well at work when their performance is not being monitored or evaluated. Interviews with employees of not-for-profit organizations suggest that the reason for their greater motivation is the belief that their work helps to improve society. Because they believe in the importance of their work, they have personal reasons to perform well, even when no financial reward is present. Thus, if our corporation began donating a significant portion of its profits to humanitarian causes, our employees' motivation and productivity would increase substantially and our overall profits would increase as well."*
>
> *Discuss how well reasoned you find this argument. In your discussion be sure to analyze the line of reasoning and the use of evidence in the argument. For example, you may need to consider what questionable Assumptions unlike the thinking and what alternative explanations or counter examples might weaken the conclusion. You can also discuss what sort of evidence would strengthen or refute the argument, what changes in the argument would make it more logically sound, and what, if anything, would help you better evaluate its conclusion.*

Strategies

A good place to start your analysis is by creating a statement that reveals the main idea of the argument. Although the writer is creating an argument, he may ultimately be stating a position, making a recommendation, or making a prediction. It may be helpful for you to determine which of these formats is most evident in the argument.

Argument

If a company donates a significant portion of its profits to humanitarian causes, its workers will become more productive and the company's overall profits will increase.

The directions for crafting your response include suggesting that you identify any questionable Assumptions that may underlie or support the writer's conclusion. The Assumptions may be stated or implied.

Claims and/or Assumptions

a) Workers in for profit organizations perform at higher levels only when they are being observed or evaluated

b) The company's workers will perform better if the company makes significant donations to humanitarian causes

c) If the company employees work harder, the company's overall profits will increase

d) Workers at nonprofits and charities are motivated by intangibles

e) Workers at the auto plant do not believe that their work is important

f) Workers at the auto manufacturing plant have displayed a lack of motivation and productivity

g) Workers at charities and nonprofits don't their time

To help you create your analysis of the argument, list alternative explanations for the claims made in the argument. What else may explain the events listed? What claims might someone on the opposite side of the argument make?

Alternative explanations and counter claims

a) Workers at nonprofits and charities may be well-paid

b) Motivation and productivity may have little to do with profitability

c) Workers at the auto manufacturing plant are still working at a for profit company

d) Workers in the auto plant may be motivated by a greater share in the profits, more benefits, more vacation time, awards, and promotions

The author of the argument may have omitted some information to make his position appear stronger. What information would help you decide if the argument has validity or what should the writer's audience know in order to make an informed decision?

Additional information needed to better evaluate the argument

a) The salaries of workers at nonprofits and charities

b) How workers at the auto plant feel about their work

c) A study of motivation in manufacturing jobs

d) The number of years on average that a worker remains at a charity or nonprofit

Sample Essay

The human resources manager has taken information from a study about worker motivation in nonprofits and applied it to the workers in the auto manufacturing plant where he or she works. The report is likely a response to concerns about worker motivation and productivity. These, in turn, may arise from lackluster or declining profits. Applying what works for a nonprofit or charity to a profit manufacturing plant may lead to frustration or disappointment for the owners.

Workers everywhere need to feel that what they do is important. According to the study cited in the argument, that is easily accomplished by workers at nonprofits and charities. The altruistic nature of the work attracts admiration from everyone. It may even be a common conception that people who work for charities and nonprofits earn far less than people in other segments of the workforce. Every charity reserves a portion of donations for administrative costs. After all, even a charity has utility bills, insurance, and employee salaries and benefits. Imagine a charity allocates a mere 10 percent of donations for administrative costs. If the donations total 5 million dollars, the charity has 500 thousand dollars with which to pay its bills and pay its employees. If there are few employees, they may each be making a healthy salary. It's easy to be highly motivated if a large paycheck comes with one's good works. Those who work for little or nothing may be students, independently wealthy, or bulking up a resume. Evaluating the employees of charities and nonprofits would be easier if the author had revealed how long they remain on the job.

Employees at the auto manufacturing company may be working there to put a roof over their heads and food on their tables. Those working on assembly lines are likely to look negatively on the idea of charity. After all, they work hard to take care of their own needs, and so should everyone else. Although they are probably not averse to helping one of their own through a tough situation, the idea of donating money to help people or causes they don't know or have an interest in is foreign to them. The writer also expresses the idea that motivation and productivity are tied to profitability. Profits accrue to a company when sales are greater than expenses. Workers in this plant can be both motivated and productive, but if the automobiles they build do not sell, there will be no profits. If demand for the autos is high, but the company cannot meet the demand because its workers are not motivated or productive, the managers must take action. They should find out what the workers need to make them feel important and not take information from an entirely different segment of the workforce.

Argument Task 21

The following appeared in the editorial section of a newspaper:

"As public concern over drug abuse has increased, authorities have become more vigilant in their efforts to prevent illegal drugs from entering the country. Many drug traffickers have consequently switched from marijuana, which is bulky, or heroin, which has a market too small to justify the risk of severe punishment, to cocaine. Thus enforcement efforts have ironically resulted in an observed increase in the illegal use of cocaine."

Discuss how well reasoned you find this argument. In your discussion be sure to analyze the line of reasoning and the use of evidence in the argument. For example, you may need to consider what questionable Assumptions unlike the thinking and what alternative explanations or counter examples might weaken the conclusion. You can also discuss what sort of evidence would strengthen or refute the argument, what changes in the argument would make it more logically sound, and what, if anything, would help you better evaluate its conclusion.

Strategies

A good place to start your analysis is by creating a statement that reveals the main idea of the argument. Although the writer is creating an argument, he may ultimately be stating a position, making a recommendation, or making a prediction. It may be helpful for you to determine which of these formats is most evident in the argument.

Argument

Increased law enforcement has led to an increase in cocaine use.

The directions for crafting your response include suggesting that you identify any questionable Assumptions that may underlie or support the writer's conclusion. The Assumptions may be stated or implied.

Claims and/or Assumptions

a) Increased vigilance has led to an overall reduction in the availability of illegal drugs

b) People are using less marijuana and heroin

c) Public concern led to increased vigilance

d) Marijuana, cocaine, and heroin are the only drugs that law enforcement and the public are concerned with

To help you create your analysis of the argument, list alternative explanations for the claims made in the argument. What else may explain the events listed? What claims might someone on the opposite side of the argument make?

Alternative explanations and/or counterclaims

a) Vigilant means watchful or alert; a better action might be diligent

b) Law enforcement was aware of the problem before the public was

c) Domestic production of marijuana is not a concern

d) Drug users have switched to cocaine as a result of shortage of other drugs

e) There has been an increase in the use of methamphetamine, prescription pain relievers, bath salts, etc

The author of the argument may have omitted some information to make his position appear stronger. What information would help you decide if the argument has validity or what should the writer's audience know in order to make an informed decision?

Additional information needed to better evaluate the argument

a) If marijuana and heroin use have declined

b) If the increase in cocaine use is sudden or ongoing

c) What is being done about domestic marijuana production?

d) If penalties have become more severe

Sample Essay

The use of the word vigilance is both vague and troubling. Vigilance is watchfulness. The reader might question if vigilance is the only action that law enforcement is taking. It would be helpful to know if the enforcement efforts include stiffer penalties for drug traffickers, including higher fines and longer jail terms. Little is said in the argument about overall drug use. The author's only claim is that cocaine use has increased. One might question if this effect has indeed been caused by a reduction in the use of other drugs.

Marijuana is easy to grow virtually anywhere. Its nickname, weed, reveals its nature. Weeds don't need any special care to thrive and flourish. The only challenge for domestic growers is hiding the growing plants from the authorities, and some accomplish that by setting up growing rooms in their homes or basements. News stories reveal that marijuana has replace alcohol as most teens' drug of choice. This growing market makes the financial benefit of growing marijuana worth the risk of detection. Punishments for the possession and sale of marijuana have also been reduced, and many states have decriminalized possession for personal use. Overcrowded prisons make the incidence of jail time for marijuana sales and possession increasingly rare.

The author of this editorial also fails to mention other drugs that have reared their ugly heads in the recent past and whether the authorities have taken steps to reduce their abuse. Methamphetamine use is a serious problem in towns and cities around the country. It can be manufactured from products available on the shelves of grocery and drug stores. It is highly addictive. Its manufacture in homes in neighborhoods is extremely dangerous as the process is highly explosive. This author would lead one to believe that marijuana, heroin, and cocaine are the only concerns of the public and the increased vigilance in their sale will allay those concerns. The public may, instead, be concerned about the house down the street that has more than its share of visitors at unusual hours or the strange smell emanating from it.

The observable increase in cocaine use may not be connected to increased vigilance at all. Had its use been on the increase prior to the authorities' ramping up their enforcement efforts? It would also be helpful to know why the public is concerned about drug abuse. Increased crime rates, court expenses, homelessness, absenteeism from work and school, result to some degree from drug abuse. How much of an increase has been in public concern? If that increase is significant in a short period of time, the authorities are correct in increasing their efforts to squelch the cross-border traffic. If domestic production of illegal drugs is on the rise, then watching the borders will have little effect on overall drug use and abuse. The reader needs more information before deciding that the actions of the authorities are laudable or sufficient to reassure the public.

Argument Task 22

The following appeared as part of an article in a magazine on lifestyles:

"Two years ago, City L was listed 14th in an annual survey that ranks cities according to the quality of life that can be enjoyed by those living in them. This information will enable people who are moving to the state in which City L is located to confidently identify one place, at least, where schools are good, housing is affordable, people are friendly, the environment is safe, and the arts flourish."

Discuss how well reasoned you find this argument. In your discussion be sure to analyze the line of reasoning and the use of evidence in the argument. For example, you may need to consider what questionable Assumptions unlike the thinking and what alternative explanations or counter examples might weaken the conclusion. You can also discuss what sort of evidence would strengthen or refute the argument, what changes in the argument would make it more logically sound, and what, if anything, would help you better evaluate its conclusion.

Strategies

A good place to start your analysis is by creating a statement that reveals the main idea of the argument. Although the writer is creating an argument, he may ultimately be stating a position, making a recommendation, or making a prediction. It may be helpful for you to determine which of these formats is most evident in the argument.

Argument - implied

City L ranks high for overall quality of life.

The directions for crafting your response include suggesting that you identify any questionable Assumptions that may underlie or support the writer's conclusion. The Assumptions may be stated or implied.

Claims and/or Assumptions

a) City L has ranked high in a survey of quality of life

b) Good schools, affordable housing, friendly people, safety, and a flourishing art scene are the requirements for a good quality of life

c) A large number of cities were included in the survey

d) The survey is intended to encourage people to relocate to City L

e) The survey included opinions of people who live in City L

To help you create your analysis of the argument, list alternative explanations for the claims made in the argument. What else may explain the events listed? What claims might someone on the opposite side of the argument make?

Alternative explanations or counter claims

a) The survey included a small number of cities

b) The number of criteria evaluated is limited

c) The magazine may have used demographic information from the city's website and not actual interviews of city residents

The author of the argument may have omitted some information to make his position appear stronger. What information would help you decide if the argument has validity or what should the writer's audience know in order to make an informed decision?

Additional information needed to better evaluate the argument

a) How many cities were included in the survey?

b) Other criteria important to people relocating - health care, jobs

c) The magazine's target audience

d) How cities were selected for the survey

e) How the magazine conducted the survey

Sample Essay

A number of caveats should be observed when reading the results of any survey. The questions are likely designed to elicit certain types of responses. Virtually everyone has been asked to respond to a telephone survey and have been frustrated by the limited number of acceptable responses enumerated by the survey administrator. When reading the results of the survey cited in this argument, one should be aware that the types of questions and responses may have been manipulated by the organization that commissioned the survey.

The first questionable element in the argument is that the author cites a survey from two years ago to recommend the livability of City L. Because it is an annual survey, those who are considering relocating might question where City L ranks in the most recent version. Any number of events may have occurred in the two years since the cited survey. For example, a small town in northern Maine relied on a nearby Air Force base to fill 85 percent of the desks in its local middle and high schools. The decision was made in 1991 to close the base, and, by the fall of 1994, the last of the personnel had left the installation. Imagine how different the responses about livability would have been in 1991 compared to 1994. All of the town's students are now housed in a single building and course offerings have been reduced. Housing is affordable because so more houses are for sale than there are buyers for them. It is still a safe, friendly town, but there is little in the way of the arts for its citizens to experience. Military base closures don't affect a large number of towns across the country, but factory's closing or natural disasters like tornadoes and hurricanes can also have devastating effect on a city in a short period of time.

Another claim that requires inspection is the 14th-place ranking of City L. This is significant if a large number of cities were included in the survey. Being 14th out of 100 is impressive; being 14th out of 20 is disappointing. The author does not tell us if the ranking cited is an improvement from earlier surveys, or if City L has experienced drop in the rankings. People moving there may be getting in on an upswing in City L's fortunes or witnessing a reversal of fortunes there.Last but not least is the intended audience for the magazine in which the survey results appears. Because the quality of schools is mentioned, one might assume that the magazine targets families with children. On the other hand, there is no mention of the employment possibilities in City L. The availability of good jobs would be an important consideration for young families. Empty nesters or retirees would find friendliness, safety, affordable housing, and a flourishing arts scene appealing but may find good schools a superfluous amenity.

City L may, indeed, be a fine place to relocate in the state. Those considering it based on the results of this survey should ask about the missing information before making an expensive move or a costly mistake.

Argument Task 23

> *The following appeared in a newspaper editorial:*
>
> *"As violence in movies increases, so do crime rates increases in our cities. To combat this problem we must establish a board to censor certain movies, or we must limit admission to persons over 21 years of age. Apparently our legislators are not concerned about this issue since a bill calling for such actions recently failed to receive a majority vote."*
>
> *Discuss how well reasoned you find this argument. In your discussion be sure to analyze the line of reasoning and the use of evidence in the argument. For example, you may need to consider what questionable Assumptions unlike the thinking and what alternative explanations or counter examples might weaken the conclusion. You can also discuss what sort of evidence would strengthen or refute the argument, what changes in the argument would make it more logically sound, and what, if anything, would help you better evaluate its conclusion.*

Strategies

A good place to start your analysis is by creating a statement that reveals the main idea of the argument. Although the writer is creating an argument, he may ultimately be stating a position, making a recommendation, or making a prediction. It may be helpful for you to determine which of these formats is most evident in the argument.

Argument

Legislators displayed their lack of concern about increased violence by failing to create a censorship board.

The directions for crafting your response include suggesting that you identify any questionable Assumptions that may underlie or support the writer's conclusion. The Assumptions may be stated or implied.

Claims and/or Assumptions

a)   Violence in movies has a direct correlation in the crime rate

b)   People over 21 are not negatively affected by violence in movies

c)   Failure to pass a bill indicates a lack of concern among legislators

d)   More violent crimes are committed as violence in movies increases

To help you create your analysis of the argument, list alternative explanations for the claims made in the argument. What else may explain the events listed? What claims might someone on the opposite side of the argument make?

Alternative explanations and counter claims

a)   Crimes rates outside of the cities have not increased

b)   Legislators disagreed with the definition of violence

c) Legislators disagreed with the age restriction

The author of the argument may have omitted some information to make his position appear stronger. What information would help you decide if the argument has validity or what should the writer's audience know in order to make an informed decision?

Additional information needed to evaluate the argument

a) The types of crimes that are on the increase

b) Who is committing the majority of the crimes?

c) How close the actual vote was

d) Whether there are more movies containing violence or if movies in that genre are depicting more violence than they previously have

Sample Essay

The author of this editorial may be two coincidental events and tying them together with a weak cause-and-effect line of reasoning. he believes that since there is more violence in movies and more crime in the cities at the same time, then the movie violence must be responsible for the elevated crime rate. Furthermore, he condemns the legislators who failed to vote in favor of a bill that would either censor some movies or restrict attendance to those over 21 years of age. There are omissions in the argument that prevent the reader from fairly evaluating its merit.

The first glaring omission is a recounting of the types of crimes that have increased in frequency. The author of the editorial does not make clear whether or not there has been an increase in violent crimes which one would assume to be the correlation to violence in movies. Can increased violence in movies be held responsible for rising rates of theft, burglary, purse snatchings, vandalism, etc? It could even be true that in the overall crime rate that there are fewer crimes of violence.

In the United States there already exists a rating system for movies, some of which are intended for parents to use when deciding which movies their children can see and others that ban children under the age of 17 from attending. The recommendation to establish a board to censor certain movies or to restrict those younger than 21 from attending is redundant. It may also be impractical to prevent citizens who can vote, serve in the military, and borrow money at the age of 18 from seeing certain movies. One can imagine protests at state capitols around the country. This may have been a consideration in the legislature's reluctance to create a censorship board.

When calculating increased violence in movies, the reader should ask to know if there are a greater number of violent movies being released, or is there greater violence in a similar number of movies each year. If more violent movies are being produced and released, it may be cause for concern as more people will be exposed to them. If the number of movies has not increased but each one depicts more violence, it is not as likely that more viewers will be exposed to the violence. More control of viewing might be achieved by limiting the number of movies containing gratuitous violence that are released by studios each year.

The type of violence depicted in movies is also a consideration. Movies containing violence against women or children could be considered more disturbing than movies depicting the violence of war. Realistic violent scenes show the actual consequences of violent acts and may serve as warnings. Violence in science fiction or fantasy films may lead younger viewers to lack empathy for the victims of violence, and it could be argues that these movies need stronger warnings.

Based on the writer's failure to make a clear connection between violence in movies and violence in real life, the reader should not hurry to condemn the legislators' decision to vote in the negative concerning a censorship board or restrict entrance to the movies to those 21 or over. If the writer could establish a relationship between movies and real life or cite statistics revealing that children under 21 are committing more violent crimes, the readers may accept the editorial as a call to action.

Argument Task 24

The following was excerpted from the speech of a spokesperson for Synthetic Farm Products, Inc.:

"Many farmers who invested in the equipment needed to make the switch from synthetic to organic fertilizers and pesticides feel that it would be too expensive to resume synthetic farming at this point. But studies of farmers who switched to organic farming last year indicate that their current crop yields are lower. Hence their purchase of organic farming equipment, a relatively minor investment compared to the losses that would result from continued lower crop yields, cannot justify persisting on an unwise course. And the choice to farm organically is financially unwise, given that it was motivated by environmental rather than economic concerns."

Discuss how well reasoned you find this argument. In your discussion be sure to analyze the line of reasoning and the use of evidence in the argument. For example, you may need to consider what questionable Assumptions unlike the thinking and what alternative explanations or counter examples might weaken the conclusion. You can also discuss what sort of evidence would strengthen or refute the argument, what changes in the argument would make it more logically sound, and what, if anything, would help you better evaluate its conclusion.

Strategies

A good place to start your analysis is by creating a statement that reveals the main idea of the argument. Although the writer is creating an argument, he may ultimately be stating a position, making a recommendation, or making a prediction. It may be helpful for you to determine which of these formats is most evident in the argument.

Argument - implied

Organic farmers can make more money by switching to synthetic equipment.

The directions for crafting your response include suggesting that you identify any questionable Assumptions that may underlie or support the writer's conclusion. The Assumptions may be stated or implied.

Claims and/or Assumptions

a) Organic fertilizers create lower crop yields

b) Organic farming is not economically viable

c) Organic farmers base their choices on environmental concerns

d) In order to make money, organic farmers should return to synthetic farm products

e) Organic farming equipment cannot be used to farm with synthetic products

f) Organic crops demand the same prices as crops grown with synthetic products

To help you create your analysis of the argument, list alternative explanations for the claims made in the argument. What else may explain the events listed? What claims might someone on the opposite side of the argument make?

Alternative explanations and counter claims

a) Factors other than fertilizers can contribute to lower crop yields

b) Organic crops command higher prices

c) Many organic farmers live in an area that experienced a severe drought last year

The author of the argument may have omitted some information to make his position appear stronger. What information would help you decide if the argument has validity or what should the writer's audience know in order to make an informed decision?

Additional information needed to better evaluate the argument

a) Climate conditions during the year in question

b) The prices commanded by organic crops in comparison to conventionally grown crops

c) The success rate of organic farmers who have been growing crops for several years

Sample Essay

The spokesperson for a company that will suffer financially if a large number of farmers switch to organic methods and products is liable to skew the facts to suit the company's purpose. The additional fact that the speaker used the results from one year of farming is further cause for caution when examining this argument. The author's principal aim appears to make others believe that organic farming is emotionally satisfying but not financially rewarding.

The audience needs more information about the organic farmers mentioned in the speech. It would seem that the speaker is referring to farmers who have been growing organically for a number of years as well as those who switched to organic farming last year. The newer growers appear to be disappointed with their yields from last year. One might extrapolate from this that the more experienced farmers had better yields. Another way to look at these seemingly true statements is to agree that crop yields are consistently lower for organic rather than synthetic farmers, but the money commanded by organic products is enough to offset the reduction in yield. Alternatively, the lower yields may not be typical. However, there may be a perfectly rational explanation for them. Bountiful crops rely on great weather conditions. There may have been too little rain or too much rain; the temperatures may have been too high or they may have been too low. There may have been an early frost. Whatever the reason, one season should not decide one's future as an organic farmer.

Farming is a business, and, even though many in the business may have chosen it because of environmental concerns, those growers still have bills to pay and a living to make. The requirements for a farm to be certified as organic are stringent, and farmers are not apt to make the decision lightly. These farmers are as likely as conventional farmers to have done considerable research about the best crops to grow for their particular soil and climate conditions in order to ensure financial success. Based on the proliferation of organically grown fruits and vegetables and organically raised meat products that have appeared in grocery stores over the past few years, those farmers have made the right decision.

The reader knows who the speaker is for this argument, but the composition of the audience is not revealed. The audience may be filled with Synthetic Farm Products dealers from around the country in an effort to motivate them to sell more products. He may be speaking to growers who are considering the switch from traditional to organic farming. Whatever the case, the speech is self-promoting, and the listener must attend with a degree of skepticism.

Argument Task 25

The following appeared as part of the business plan of an investment and financial consulting firm:

"Studies suggest that an average coffee drinker's consumption of coffee increases with age, from age 10 through ages 60. Even after age 60, coffee consumption remains high. The average cola drinker's consumption of cola, however, declines with increasing age. Both of these trends have remained stable for the past 40 years. Given that the number of older adults will significantly increase as the population ages over the next 20 years, it follows that the demand for coffee will increase and the demand for cola will decrease during this period. We should, therefore, consider transferring our investments from Cola Loca to Early Bird Coffee."

Discuss how well reasoned you find this argument. In your discussion be sure to analyze the line of reasoning and the use of evidence in the argument. For example, you may need to consider what questionable Assumptions unlike the thinking and what alternative explanations or counter examples might weaken the conclusion. You can also discuss what sort of evidence would strengthen or refute the argument, what changes in the argument would make it more logically sound, and what, if anything, would help you better evaluate its conclusion.

Strategies

A good place to start your analysis is by creating a statement that reveals the main idea of the argument. Although the writer is creating an argument, he may ultimately be stating a position, making a recommendation, or making a prediction. It may be helpful for you to determine which of these formats is most evident in the argument.

Recommendation

The investment and financial consulting firm recommends transferring investments from Cola Loca to Early Bird Coffee.

The directions for crafting your response include suggesting that you identify any questionable Assumptions that may underlie or support the writer's conclusion. The Assumptions may be stated or implied.

Claims and/or Assumptions

a) The rate of coffee drinking increases from age10 to age 60

b) The rate of cola consumption declines with the age of the consumer

c) Throughout an individual's lifetime, he will consume more coffee than cola

To help you create your analysis of the argument, list alternative explanations for the claims made in the argument. What else may explain the events listed? What claims might someone on the opposite side of the argument make?

Alternative explanations and/or counter claims

a)   The greatest rate of increase in coffee drinking is likely to occur between the ages of 20 and 30 years of age and remain fairly steady after that

b)   Consumers are likely to spend more years of their life drinking cola than drinking coffee

The author of the argument may have omitted some information to make his position appear stronger. What information would help you decide if the argument has validity or what should the writer's audience know in order to make an informed decision?

Additional information needed to better evaluate the argument

a)   The rates of increase and decline in coffee and cola consumption as consumer's age

b)   The ages at which the increase and decline occur most dramatically

c)   The P/E ratio for each company

d)   Overall spending on each beverage per year

Sample Essay

An investment and financial consulting firm is considering transferring its investments from Cola Loca to Early Bird Coffee. Because they are working with money entrusted to them by their clients, they must consider all of the ramifications of this move. Their purpose, after all, is to make money for their clients. Based on the statements in the argument, the reader does not know if one company is more profitable and, therefore, more likely to pay dividends.

This business plan uses demographics as the chief support for the recommendation, citing consumption of coffee and cola by age group. It is interesting that the author has used the ages from 10 through 60 to demonstrate the increase in coffee consumption. It is highly unlikely that 10-year-olds are drinking coffee at all, let alone enough to be included in this statistic. In fact, the greatest increase in coffee consumption may occurs between the ages of 10 and 20 with the bulk of that occurring between the ages of 18 and 20 as young people leave home for college or the workplace. The rate of increased consumption between the ages of 20 to 60 may be very slight and probably levels off very soon after the age of 20, so that age range would not have produced convincing numbers. While those between the ages of 10 and 18 are probably not drinking much coffee, they probably are drinking a lot of cola. The author's choice to omit an age range for increased cola consumption makes it more difficult for the reader to fairly compare the two beverages.

The reader is not given information about the age at which cola consumption begins to remain steady. It also may happen at age 60, with no significant decline after that. One also does not know when consumption of cola begins to increase, which might be at age 10, or at what age it begins to decline. An argument can be made that the decline in soda consumption doesn't begin until age 40, or 50, or 60. Everything a out cola consumption is so speculative that it seems deceptive to use it as a foundation of the recommendation. Based on the ambiguity, it is also difficult to take seriously the claims about future sizes of different age groups as a rationale for the suggested investment. It may be that increases and declines in both coffee and cola consumption cross each other at a midpoint in the same age range, making the total consumptions of each virtually equal.

Ultimately, an investment decision should be based on the bottom line. This investment and financial consulting firm must look at the history of sales for each company. Are sales increasing, declining, stagnant? How well is each company managed? In the final analysis, the company worthy of investment must be profitable as the stockholders will expect dividends on their investment.

Argument Task 26

> The following is part of a business plan being discussed at a board meeting of the Perks Company:
>
> "It is no longer cost-effective for the Perks Company to continue offering its employees a generous package of benefits and incentives year after year. In periods when national unemployment rates are low, Perks may need to offer such a package in order to attract and keep good employees, but since national unemployment rates are now high, Perks does not need to offer the same benefits and incentives. The money thus saved could be better used to replace the existing plant machinery with more technologically sophisticated equipment, or even to build an additional plant."
>
> Discuss how well reasoned you find this argument. In your discussion be sure to analyze the line of reasoning and the use of evidence in the argument. For example, you may need to consider what questionable Assumptions unlike the thinking and what alternative explanations or counter examples might weaken the conclusion. You can also discuss what sort of evidence would strengthen or refute the argument, what changes in the argument would make it more logically sound, and what, if anything, would help you better evaluate its conclusion.

Strategies

A good place to start your analysis is by creating a statement that reveals the main idea of the argument. Although the writer is creating an argument, he may ultimately be stating a position, making a recommendation, or making a prediction. It may be helpful for you to determine which of these formats is most evident in the argument.

Argument

The Perks Company should shift money from employee benefits for use to replace plant machinery or to build an additional plant.

The directions for crafting your response include suggesting that you identify any questionable Assumptions that may underlie or support the writer's conclusion. The Assumptions may be stated or implied.

Claims and/or Assumptions

a) The unemployment rate should determine the level of benefits offered to workers

b) It is no longer cost-effective for Perks to offer benefits and incentives

c) The cost of benefits and incentives outweighs the advantage of retaining good employees

d) Money saved by reducing or eliminating benefits and incentives can be used to replace existing machinery money saved by reducing or eliminating benefits and incentives can be used to build an additional plant

To help you create your analysis of the argument, list alternative explanations for the claims made in the

argument. What else may explain the events listed? What claims might someone on the opposite side of the argument make?

Alternative explanations and/or counter claims

a) The quality of the workers may decline if Perks eliminates benefits and incentives

b) When employment is high around the country, Perks employees may leave the company for a job with benefits

c) Providing or eliminating benefits when employment rates change makes it difficult create a long-range plan for the company

d) Perks employees may have skills that make them desirable hires regardless of employment numbers

e) Investing in new technology may make employees more efficient, saving money on overtime or creating more product to fill orders

The author of the argument may have omitted some information to make his position appear stronger. What information would help you decide if the argument has validity or what should the writer's audience know in order to make an informed decision?

Additional information needed to better evaluate the argument

a) What effect incentives have on employee work habits?

b) Other changes that company can make to save money

c) The cost of training new employees

d) If Perks employees are unionized and working under a binding contract

Sample Essay

An employee cost is one of the few expenses that a company can control. The state and/or federal government determine property and employment taxes. Lenders determine the amount of insurance a company must carry. The utilities companies determine the rates for electricity, heating, phone, Internet, or other amenities that help the business run smoothly. Customers or clients determine how much product or service the company must produce. When a company like Perks seeks to reduce costs, the easiest place to do so is in the number of employees they hire or what pay and benefits they provide for their employees. Because it is the simplest way to reduce costs does not make it the most advisable way to do so, even when high unemployment provides what may be a large pool of prospective employees.

Salaries and benefits for employees are a significant expense for any company, and, when times are tough, it is tempting for management to make cuts there. Before Perks eliminates benefits and incentives, the company must consider the ramifications. Their employees may have skills that remains marketable even in a tough economy and may feel confident that they can easily find work elsewhere if conditions become untenable at Perks. The cost of training new employees may be greater than the cost of retaining its current workers. During the training period, Perks could fall behind in filling orders causing customers or clients to find other sources, and Perks will lose money. This snowball effect can be devastating.

One of the company's goals is to replace existing machinery with more technologically-advanced equipment, an expense that should be in a company's long-range plan if it wants to continue to compete in a fast-paced environment. Retaining its current, highly-trained employees and obtaining a loan for equipment that will help them manufacture the Perks product more quickly at a higher quality may be the more cost-effective route for the company. Capital expenditures are generally not made at the expense of the workforce. On the other hand, better machinery may make it possible for Perks to reduce its workforce while retaining benefits and incentives for those who remain. Building another plant is economically sound only if demand for Perks products has increased significantly or demand for their products is predicted to rise over the next few years. The concomitant expense will be hiring and training new employees.

It may be, in fact, impossible to eliminate employee benefits and incentives. If Perks' workers are unionized, they may be working under a binding contract that stipulates rates of pay, periodic raises, benefits and incentives for proficiency. The company may have to take extreme measures that include paying expensive legal bills to break the contract. There may even be a strike clause in the contract, and Perks could find production shut down if the workers strike in protest over the proposed changes.

A good business plan considers past actions and attempts to predict future activity based on market conditions, demand for its products or services, obsolescence of physical plants and machinery, along with the cost of employees. It may be short-sighted to base future profitability on the backs of its current, apparently effective workers.

Argument Task 27

The following appeared as part of a recommendation from the financial planning office to the administration of Fern Valley University:

"In the past few years, Fern Valley University has suffered from a decline in both enrollments and admissions applications. The reason can be discovered from our students, who most often cite poor teaching and inadequate library resources as their chief sources of dissatisfaction with Fern Valley. Therefore, in order to increase the number of students attending our university, and hence to regain our position as the most prestigious university in the greater Fern Valley metropolitan area, it is necessary to initiate a fund-raising campaign among the alumni that will enable us to expand the range of subjects we teach and to increase the size of our library facilities."

Discuss how well reasoned you find this argument. In your discussion be sure to analyze the line of reasoning and the use of evidence in the argument. For example, you may need to consider what questionable Assumptions unlike the thinking and what alternative explanations or counter examples might weaken the conclusion. You can also discuss what sort of evidence would strengthen or refute the argument, what changes in the argument would make it more logically sound, and what, if anything, would help you better evaluate its conclusion.

Strategies

A good place to start your analysis is by creating a statement that reveals the main idea of the argument. Although the writer is creating an argument, he may ultimately be stating a position, making a recommendation, or making a prediction. It may be helpful for you to determine which of these formats is most evident in the argument.

Argument

Fern Valley University must initiate a fund-raising campaign among its alumni to expand the range of subjects taught and to increase the size of the library facilities.

The directions for crafting your response include suggesting that you identify any questionable Assumptions that may underlie or support the writer's conclusion. The Assumptions may be stated or implied.

Claims and/or Assumptions

   a)   Fern Valley University has experienced a decline in enrollment and admissions applications

   b)   Poor teaching and inadequate library facilities are the source of the decline

   c)   FVU has been the most prestigious university in the greater Fern Valley metropolitan area

   d)   There are other universities in the area

   e)   An alumni fund-raising effort is necessary to make the necessary changes

f)   FVU should expand the range of courses it teaches

g)   FVU wants to increase the number of students attending

To help you create your analysis of the argument, list alternative explanations for the claims made in the argument. What else may explain the events listed? What claims might someone on the opposite side of the argument make?

Alternative explanations and counterclaims

a)   Fern Valley University is facing tougher competition from other schools

b)   Poor teaching cannot be remedied by offering more courses

The author of the argument may have omitted some information to make his position appear stronger. What information would help you decide if the argument has validity or what should the writer's audience know in order to make an informed decision?

Additional information needed to better evaluate the argument

a)   If other universities in the area have experienced similar declines, or if they have had increases in enrollment and applicants

b)   Other sources of dissatisfaction with students

c)   What steps the university has taken to improve teaching

d)   Marketing strategies in place to attract students

e)   When the bulk of the decline occurred

Sample Essay

I once had a college professor who said, "You can't make a bad meatloaf better by making it bigger." The financial planning office at Fern Valley University believes that expanding the range of subjects it teaches and increasing the size of its library facilities will return it to the prominence it once had and attract more students. The administration would be smarter to look at this "meatloaf's" ingredients before making it bigger. Traditional colleges and universities are facing challenges from community colleges, trade schools, and online institutions and must pay attention to details they may have been able to overlook in the past.

One concern identified by students is poor teaching. The university's response appears to be offering an expanded range of courses. The reader is left to wonder if the school's hiring policies will enable them to find qualified, good teachers to fill the new positions that will be created. What will become of the courses that are currently judged as having poor instruction? Students who need those classes to complete their majors may find it more fulfilling to sit at home in their pajamas and take an online course. If that works for them, they may decide to withdraw from the university altogether. Fern Valley University might profit from looking at how it evaluates and chooses to retain its instructors. In my own experience, I know that college students often select classes based on who is teaching it. Admired professors may resent having a heavier student load because students avoid some of their colleagues. A less expensive and time consuming solution to the issue would be to replace those delivering poor instruction.

A second concern cited in the recommendation is inadequate library resources. The financial planning office has interpreted this to mean that the library is too small. Technological advances have changed how students use libraries. Students at Fern Valley University may find that the library has too few computers or a poor selection of scholarly databases needed for research. The printers may be too slow. The library may not subscribe to relevant periodicals. The administration needs more detailed information about the library's deficiencies before asking the alumni association to raise funds for an expansion.

These two issues that students have identified may not have anything to do with the decline in enrollment and applications for admission. In fact, those are problems for current students at FVU. The administration must look at other reasons for the reduction in new students. As the price of a traditional college education has risen beyond the ability of families to pay for it, high school seniors have begun looking for alternatives. Many careers in technology offer plentiful job opportunities after a shorter and less expensive period of education and/or training. Fern Valley University should evaluate the majors that it currently offers. Administration may be able to eliminate some underutilized areas of study and replace them with majors that entering freshmen find more appealing.

Whatever FVU decides, it should carefully consider student complaints. Before raising money to expand a university that already suffers from a decline in student numbers, administration must find smarter ways to fix this "meatloaf".

Argument Task 28

> *The following appeared in an article in a college departmental newsletter:*
>
> *"Professor Taylor of Jones University is promoting a model of foreign language instruction in which students receive 10 weeks of intensive training, then go abroad to live with families for 10 weeks. The superiority of the model, Professor Taylor contends, is proved by the results of a study in which foreign language tests given to students at 25 other colleges show that first-year foreign language students at Jones speak more fluently after only 10 to 20 weeks in the program than do nine out of 10 foreign language majors elsewhere at the time of their graduation."*
>
> *Discuss how well reasoned you find this argument. In your discussion be sure to analyze the line of reasoning and the use of evidence in the argument. For example, you may need to consider what questionable Assumptions unlike the thinking and what alternative explanations or counter examples might weaken the conclusion. You can also discuss what sort of evidence would strengthen or refute the argument, what changes in the argument would make it more logically sound, and what, if anything, would help you better evaluate its conclusion.*

Strategies

A good place to start your analysis is by creating a statement that reveals the main idea of the argument. Although the writer is creating an argument, he may ultimately be stating a position, making a recommendation, or making a prediction. It may be helpful for you to determine which of these formats is most evident in the argument.

Argument

Professor Taylor's method of foreign language instruction at Jones University surpasses the method used at other universities.

The directions for crafting your response include suggesting that you identify any questionable Assumptions that may underlie or support the writer's conclusion. The Assumptions may be stated or implied.

Claims and /or Assumptions

a)   The audience for the newsletter is other foreign language teachers

b)   Other professors of foreign language at Jones do not use Taylor's approach

To help you create your analysis of the argument, list alternative explanations for the claims made in the argument. What else may explain the events listed? What claims might someone on the opposite side of the argument make?

Alternative explanations and/ or counterclaims

a)   First-year students at other universities compare favorably to Jones first-year students

b) The newsletter is not at Jones University

The author of the argument may have omitted some information to make his position appear stronger. What information would help you decide if the argument has validity or what should the writer's audience know in order to make an informed decision?

Additional Information needed to better evaluate the argument

a) How Jones University students score on the test at graduation

b) If other colleges use the Taylor model and how those student's compare

c) If the model is used by the turns every year of their college career

d) If it applies to all languages

e) How first-year students at other universities compare to Jones' first-year students

f) How Taylor selected the 25 other schools

Sample Essay

It appears that professors at a college other than Jones University are considering a new approach to foreign language instruction. Professor Taylor recommends his own approach which involves 10 weeks of intensive training followed by 10 weeks of living abroad with families for his students. He based his recommendation on a study that compares his first-year students' fluency with the fluency of students about to graduate from 25 other universities. The results seem to scream approbation for Taylor's method, but other universities should examine them more closely before changing what they already do.

The first thing those at other schools should ask to see is how Professor Taylor's first-year students compare with the 25 other schools' first-year students. Those universities may have a first-year approach and curriculum that is equally effective in the short term. Unless Jones University students repeat the initial curriculum in consecutive years of their foreign-language studies, their fluency may decline. Jones University foreign language majors approaching graduation should be compared to students at the same level at other schools. More advanced foreign language students have likely moved on from learning to actually speak the language to studying its literature; the focus has changed. Speaking a language fluently is not necessarily the goal of every foreign language student. After graduation, some students may use their knowledge to translate legal documents for a law firm or teach at an elementary school.

The reader may assume that extensive training refers to language instruction, but the argument does not make that clear. Perhaps it involves training in cultural acclimation, familiarization with the currency, food, religion, etc. If it is strictly language instruction, Professor Taylor needs to make clear what form it takes before others can imagine using it. It may involve pedagogy that other universities are already using, and the professors there may find it easy to adapt the rest of Taylor's system. Alternatively, it may be impractical to adapt his system at some schools. Large universities with great numbers of foreign language students may find it impossible to acquire enough families to host its students for 10 weeks.

How many studies have been completed that compares Taylor's students to students from other universities? The results are reliable only if they can be duplicated over time. Those reading the newsletter article should not rush to judgment. If the goal of any college education is for students to obtain employment in their fields of study, the number of graduates achieving that should be the barometer of a program's success. Test results are useful only for demonstrating competence in what they measure. In this case, the test measure fluency in speaking a foreign language. The test should be administered every year in the student's education to measure the sustainability of that fluency to establish reliability.

Argument Task 29

> *The following appeared in an Avia Airlines departmental memorandum:*
>
> *"On average, 9 out of every 1,000 passengers who traveled on Avia Airlines last year filed a complaint about our baggage-handling procedures. This means that although some 1 percent of our passengers were unhappy with those procedures, the overwhelming majority were quite satisfied with them; thus it would appear that a review of the procedures is not important to our goal of maintaining or increasing the number of Avia's passengers."*
>
> *Discuss how well reasoned you find this argument. In your discussion be sure to analyze the line of reasoning and the use of evidence in the argument. For example, you may need to consider what questionable Assumptions unlike the thinking and what alternative explanations or counter examples might weaken the conclusion. You can also discuss what sort of evidence would strengthen or refute the argument, what changes in the argument would make it more logically sound, and what, if anything, would help you better evaluate its conclusion.*

Strategies

A good place to start your analysis is by creating a statement that reveals the main idea of the argument. Although the writer is creating an argument, he may ultimately be stating a position, making a recommendation, or making a prediction. It may be helpful for you to determine which of these formats is most evident in the argument.

Argument

A review of Avia Airlines' baggage- handling procedures is not important to the airline's goal of maintaining or increasing the number of passengers.

The directions for crafting your response include suggesting that you identify any questionable Assumptions that may underlie or support the writer's conclusion. The Assumptions may be stated or implied.

Claims and/or Assumptions

a) Only one percent of passengers complained about luggage-handling procedures

b) Avia Airlines believes that the small number of complaints will not affect the number of passengers that choose or stay with the airline

To help you create your analysis of the argument, list alternative explanations for the claims made in the argument. What else may explain the events listed? What claims might someone on the opposite side of the argument make?

Alternative explanations and/or counterclaims

a) Not every dissatisfied passenger files a complaint.

b) The complaints all occurred at the same airport

The author of the argument may have omitted some information to make his position appear stronger. What information would help you decide if the argument has validity or what should the writer's audience know in order to make an informed decision?

Additional information needed to better evaluate the argument

   a)   The types of complaints that the company received

   b)   At which airports the complaints occurred

   c)   On which flights the complaints occurred

   d)   The time period during which the complains occurred

Sample Essay

Based on the information provided in this memorandum, the reader would agree that Avia Airlines has a very minor problem with baggage-handling procedures. In fact, virtually any company would be pleased if complaints occurred at a mere one percent rate. More details about the complaints here might reveal a specific issue with Avia Airlines, causing the reader to change his or her mind. Is it wise for any company to examine its policies and procedures carefully on a regular basis and determine the causes of complaints and seek remedies?

Avia Airlines should first determine if the bulk of the complaints occur at one airport or if they are evenly distributed among the airports into which the airline flies. If the complaints are scattered about, they are probably nothing to be concerned about. However, if most of them occur at one airport, the airline must discover the reason. Maybe, all airlines have concerns at the same airport. It may have to do with the configuration of the physical plant or the personnel, but steps must be taken by the managers of the airport itself to keep the airlines from pulling out and selecting another airport. If the problem is with the baggage handlers, they may need further training. The regular baggage handlers could be on strike and replacements are doing the job. The issue may even be narrowed down to a specific flight each day. Perhaps that flight arrives just before or after a shift change or when the airport is most congested. Any of these conditions must be pointed out and rectified.

Nine complaints per thousand is, indeed, a small number, but, if the airline flies five thousand passengers per day, the cumulative number of passengers with complaints is 45. If the airline flies the same number of passengers every day of the year, the total number is over sixteen thousand complaints. When percentages are translated into real numbers, they create a different impression. It would be helpful to know how long it takes an employee of the airline to handle each complaint. If the manger multiplies the number of hours spent in this endeavor by the hourly wage of the employee(s), he may be shocked at the expense involved. If the expense is great enough, it may affect other aspects of the airline's service, which can create customers that are dissatisfied with more than just baggage handling. These customers may select another airline in the future, indeed affecting Avia's ability to maintain the same number of passengers.

Any business should be grateful for customers who make their complaints known. It is the business' opportunity to improve. Businesses also realize that the complaints they know about are usually the tip of the iceberg; many more say nothing and simply disappear. Avia must be aware of this and make the necessary changes to please both those who are dissatisfied and tell about it and those who are dissatisfied and say nothing. Disregarding the problem will eventually catch up with Avia Airlines.

Argument Task 30

> *The following appeared in an article in the health section of a newspaper:*
>
> *"There is a common misconception that university hospitals are better than community or private hospitals. This notion is unfounded, however: the university hospitals in our region employ 15 percent fewer doctors, have a 20 percent lower success rate in treating patients, make far less overall profit, and pay their medical staff considerably less than do private hospitals. Furthermore, many doctors at university hospitals typically divide their time among teaching, conducting research, and treating patients. From this it seems clear that the quality of care at university hospitals is lower than that at other kinds of hospitals."*
>
> *Discuss how well reasoned you find this argument. In your discussion be sure to analyze the line of reasoning and the use of evidence in the argument. For example, you may need to consider what questionable Assumptions unlike the thinking and what alternative explanations or counter examples might weaken the conclusion. You can also discuss what sort of evidence would strengthen or refute the argument, what changes in the argument would make it more logically sound, and what, if anything, would help you better evaluate its conclusion.*

Strategies

A good place to start your analysis is by creating a statement that reveals the main idea of the argument. Although the writer is creating an argument, he may ultimately be stating a position, making a recommendation, or making a prediction. It may be helpful for you to determine which of these formats is most evident in the argument.

Argument

The quality of care at university hospitals is lower than that at other kinds of hospitals.

The directions for crafting your response include suggesting that you identify any questionable Assumptions that may underlie or support the writer's conclusion. The Assumptions may be stated or implied.

Claims and/or Assumptions

a) University hospitals in the area employ 15 percent fewer doctors

b) University hospitals in the area have a 20 percent lower success rate in treating patients

c) University hospitals in the area make far less overall profit

d) University hospitals in the area pay their medical staff considerably less than do private hospitals

e) Many doctors at university hospitals divided their time among teaching, conducting research, and treating patients

f) The doctor to patient ratio is high

g) More patients succumb to their illnesses

    h)   Medical staff is dissatisfied with their pay

    i)   Too little time is spent on patient care

To help you create your analysis of the argument, list alternative explanations for the claims made in the argument. What else may explain the events listed? What claims might someone on the opposite side of the argument make?

Alternative explanations and counter claims

    a)   University hospitals may have fewer beds and need a smaller staff

    b)   University hospitals may see more seriously ill patients than do other types of hospitals

    c)   University hospitals are nonprofit institutions

    d)   Many doctors may be residents and, therefore, are paid less

    e)   Private hospitals can choose which patients to see

    f)   University hospitals may focus on emergency medicine

The author of the argument may have omitted some information to make his position appear stronger. What information would help you decide if the argument has validity or what should the writer's audience know in order to make an informed decision?

Additional information needed to better evaluate the argument

    a)   The number of beds in each hospital

    b)   Actual number of doctors at each hospital

    c)   Doctor/patient ratio

    d)   Types of patients seen at each hospital

    e)   Actual salaries of medical staff at each hospital

Sample Essay

The reader doesn't know the source of the statement that the writer of this article is disputing. Neither is one able to determine what those misled people thinking is better about university hospitals compared to private or community hospitals. In the last sentence of the argument the writer claims that the quality of care in university hospitals is inferior to that in other types of hospitals based on supposed facts about staffing numbers, profit levels, lower success levels, and pay received by staff. Anyone seeking medical care should ask for more facts before choosing a private or community hospital over a university medical facility.

The author states that university hospitals in his area employ 15 percent fewer doctors than do the community hospitals. A more pertinent comparison would be doctor/patient ratio. For example, the community hospital has 30 doctors on staff; at 15 percent fewer, the university hospital would have 25.5 doctors on staff. If both hospitals have the same number of beds, the potential exists for each university hospital doctor to be responsible for more patients than the community hospital doctor. However, if the community hospital has a significantly greater number of beds than the university hospital, those ratios could be reversed. Doctor patient ration becomes more relevant based on the types of cases in each hospital. If the university hospital sees more critically ill patients, it would be better for those patients if each doctor were assigned fewer patients.

The type of patient admitted to each institution also affects the success rate of the hospital. Private hospitals, in fact, can choose which patients to admit, thus assuring them of a higher success rate. As public institutions, community and university hospitals must treat everyone who walks through the door. It would be more revealing to compare the various facilities based on their success rates for various specific illnesses or treatments. How do patients in each of the hospitals fare after open-heart surgery, for example? Prospective patients may only be concerned about a hospital's success rate with the procedure that has been prescribed for them. The university hospital may, in the interest of medical advances, take only the most challenging cases. One of their goals is to prepare future doctors for the types of cases they will encounter when they have moved on from the university.

An additional concern of the author is the lower profit level at the university hospital. As stated in the previous paragraph, university and public hospitals cannot turn away patients regardless of illness. Nor can they do so based on a patient's ability to pay. In addition, universities, by definition, are not profit-making institutions. They do not have stockholders who expect a return on their investment. The reader might assume that any income generated at the university hospital would go back into training future doctors or improved facilities.

This argument uses irrelevant and, perhaps, misleading information about university hospitals to bolster the writer's contention that one can receive better care at a community or private hospital. Anyone planning to undergo a complex or dangerous procedure should research hospitals based on their ability to perform successfully.

Argument Task 31

> *The following appeared as part of a column in a popular entertainment magazine:*
>
> *"The producers of the forthcoming movie 3003 will be most likely to maximize their profits if they are willing to pay Robin Good several million dollars to star in it—even though that amount is far more than any other person involved with the movie will make. After all, Robin has in the past been paid a similar amount to work in several films that were very financially successful."*
>
> *Discuss how well reasoned you find this argument. In your discussion be sure to analyze the line of reasoning and the use of evidence in the argument. For example, you may need to consider what questionable Assumptions unlike the thinking and what alternative explanations or counter examples might weaken the conclusion. You can also discuss what sort of evidence would strengthen or refute the argument, what changes in the argument would make it more logically sound, and what, if anything, would help you better evaluate its conclusion.*

Strategies

A good place to start your analysis is by creating a statement that reveals the main idea of the argument. Although the writer is creating an argument, he may ultimately be stating a position, making a recommendation, or making a prediction. It may be helpful for you to determine which of these formats is most evident in the argument.

Prediction

The producers of the movie, 3003, will maximize their profits if they pay Robin Good several million dollars to star in it.

The directions for crafting your response include suggesting that you identify any questionable Assumptions that may underlie or support the writer's conclusion. The Assumptions may be stated or implied.

Claims and/or Assumptions

   a)   Selecting the right star for a movie maximizes profits

   b)   producers should pay the star of the move far more than anyone else involved in the production

   c)   Robin Good insures financial success for a movie

To help you create your analysis of the argument, list alternative explanations for the claims made in the argument. What else may explain the events listed? What claims might someone on the opposite side of the argument make?

Alternative explanations and/or counterclaims

   a)   Robin Good has starred in movies of a specific genre

   b)   It has been several years since Robin Good starred in a successful movie

   c)   The movies that good starred in had larger budgets than 3003

The author of the argument may have omitted some information to make his position appear stronger. What information would help you decide if the argument has validity or what should the writer's audience know in order to make an informed decision?

Additional information needed to better evaluate the argument

   a)   How long ago Robin Good starred in a successful movie

   b)   The genre in which Robin Good has been successful

   c)   How much Robin Good was paid to star in movies in the past?

   d)   When the studio will release the movie

   e)   If the studio has had recent failures or successes

Sample Essay

Movies are expensive to produce, and the producers take enormous risks to draw fickle viewers to theaters across the country. They hire the best talent they can afford to work behind and in front of the camera. Post production is just as important as highly skilled technicians lay down the sound track, edit for playing length, adjust the color, and add the credits. A high-profile actor may be the ticket to high box office sales, but a number of considerations may temper the enthusiasm for a big name.

Everybody is familiar with movie franchises like Star Wars, the Indiana Jones action flicks with Harrison Ford in the lead role, and Tom Cruise as the action star in the Mission Impossible films. These actors have become so clearly identified with these roles that it is sometimes difficult for the viewing public to accept them in other roles. Conversely, should the producers attempt to place another actor in these iconic roles, the public may also choose not to attend the movies. Money spent or saved on the choice of a star does not necessarily ensure success and/or great profits for the producers of a movie. Robin Good may have been like money in the bank in the past when he starred in movies of a specific type, but that success may not transfer to the movie, 3003, if viewers have preconceived expectations about the star.

The producers should also take into consideration how long it has been since Robin Good starred in a blockbuster movie. He may be past his prime, and young moviegoers may not even know who he is. If the target audience is more mature, Robin Good may be a "good" choice of star for the movie, whatever the cost. Additionally, if Robin Good has not worked in a while, he may be willing to work for less than he has in the past, thereby saving the producers money that they can spend on other aspects of the film. Even if Robin Good turns in the performance of his life, being supported by inferior actors in secondary roles can reduce the overall quality of the movie. Additionally, insufficient funds remaining after paying Good may cause the producers to take shortcuts in postproduction, also reducing the quality of the finished product.

Does this studio have a string of recent successes, or is it desperate to produce a successful film? If the studio heads are grasping at straws to create long lines at the theaters, they may resort to hiring an expensive actor in the belief that his past successes will draw a large audience. Desperate times call for desperate measure. Spending a large chunk of the budget on an actor who may be a has-been is a big risk. Robin Good's success in the past may be in large part due to his co-stars. If the rest of the cast of 3003 is weak, Good may also deliver a lackluster performance. This studio and the film's producers must consider all of these factors before committing to Robin Good. There may be less expensive ways to ensure financial success for the film. Among them is arranging for the release of the movie to occur during the Christmas holidays, a period known for very high movie attendance. Ticket sales, after all determine the financial success of most movies.

Argument Task 32

> *The following appeared in the editorial section of a local newspaper:*
>
> *"If the paper from every morning edition of the nation's largest newspaper were collected and rendered into paper pulp that the newspaper could reuse, about 5 million trees would be saved each year. This kind of recycling is unnecessary, however, since the newspaper maintains its own forests to ensure an uninterrupted supply of paper."*
>
> *Discuss how well reasoned you find this argument. In your discussion be sure to analyze the line of reasoning and the use of evidence in the argument. For example, you may need to consider what questionable Assumptions unlike the thinking and what alternative explanations or counter examples might weaken the conclusion. You can also discuss what sort of evidence would strengthen or refute the argument, what changes in the argument would make it more logically sound, and what, if anything, would help you better evaluate its conclusion.*

Strategies

A good place to start your analysis is by creating a statement that reveals the main idea of the argument. Although the writer is creating an argument, he may ultimately be stating a position, making a recommendation, or making a prediction. It may be helpful for you to determine which of these formats is most evident in the argument.

Argument

Because the nation's largest newspaper maintains its own forests, it is not necessary for them to recycle and reuse every morning edition of the paper.

The directions for crafting your response include suggesting that you identify any questionable Assumptions that may underlie or support the writer's conclusion. The Assumptions may be stated or implied.

Claims and/or Assumptions

a) Reusing newsprint would save 5 million trees each year

b) Maintaining its own forests makes it unnecessary for the newspaper to recycle its papers

To help you create your analysis of the argument, list alternative explanations for the claims made in the argument. What else may explain the events listed? What claims might someone on the opposite side of the argument make?

Alternative examples and counterclaims

a) It is unlikely that every copy of every morning edition would be recycled

b) Recycling is environmentally responsible

c) Other newspapers would not encourage recycling

The author of the argument may have omitted some information to make his position appear stronger. What information would help you decide if the argument has validity or what should the writer's audience know in order to make an informed decision?

Additional information needed to better evaluate the argument

a) How the recycling process affects the environment

b) How many trees it takes to make the paper pulp for the newspaper

c) If recycling paper is less expensive than cutting and processing their own trees

d) How significant a savings is 5 million trees

e) How many trees in total are cut each year to make pulp for the other newspapers

Sample Essay

The author of this editorial expresses the opinion that the local newspaper doesn't need to be concerned with recycling because it maintains its own forests. On the surface, this seems a reasonable point of view. The local newspaper is acting responsibly toward the environment by managing its own trees rather than causing deforestation in places where responsible management does not occur. However, it seems that saving 5 million trees in any way possible is important for everyone.

This opinion may fall apart in the light of pollution caused by paper making as opposed to recycling and the cost involved in each process. The author does not reveal information about either. If the reader assumes that recycling is a friendlier process to the environment and the health of citizens in proximity to paper plants, the reluctance on the part of the country's largest newspaper to do so may have adverse effects on its sales to the public and environmentally-conscious advertisers. On the contrary, if recycling causes more pollution, then kudos go out to the newspaper that manages its own woodlots.

The newspaper that maintains its own woodlots still must arrange to have its trees converted to paper pulp. They most likely hire a woodcutting company to get the trees from the forest to the paper mill. Since paper mills are set up to specialize in making certain types of paper, these trees may have to travel a considerable distance to the appropriate mill. Large machinery is used in the harvesting and enormous trucks in the transport, all of which cause pollution through the burning of fossil fuels. In contrast, recycling centers bundle newspapers which are collected by trucks and taken to plants that return them to useable newsprint. Because the author doesn't reveal the cost of each process, it is impossible for the reader to evaluate the financial benefit to the newspaper that maintains its own forests over using recycled newsprint.

In the long run, the debate over managing a woodlot versus recycling may become moot. The advent of the Internet has made the printing of newspapers less important. Newspapers of any size have had to make each edition available to readers on the Internet. Citizens of a certain age can recall the local paperboy or girl who arose early each morning to deliver the daily paper so householders could peruse the news or complete the crossword puzzle with their morning coffee before heading off to work. The proliferation of television channels devoted to delivering the news along with morning news shows on the major networks has compounded the challenge for print media. This daily reading of the news now takes place on an iPad, and those who would rather hear or view it have a multitude of channels from which to choose.

Argument Task 33

> *The following appeared in a memorandum from the information technology department of a major advertising firm:*
>
> *"The more efficient a firm's employees are, the more profitable that firm will be. Improvements in a firm's information technology hardware and software are a proven way to increase the efficiency of employees who do the majority of their work on computers. Therefore, if our firm invests in the most powerful and advanced information technology available, employee productivity will be maximized. This strategy ensures that every dollar spent on enhanced information technology will help to increase our firm's profit margins."*
>
> *Discuss how well reasoned you find this argument. In your discussion be sure to analyze the line of reasoning and the use of evidence in the argument. For example, you may need to consider what questionable Assumptions unlike the thinking and what alternative explanations or counter examples might weaken the conclusion. You can also discuss what sort of evidence would strengthen or refute the argument, what changes in the argument would make it more logically sound, and what, if anything, would help you better evaluate its conclusion.*

Strategies

A good place to start your analysis is by creating a statement that reveals the main idea of the argument. Although the writer is creating an argument, he may ultimately be stating a position, making a recommendation, or making a prediction. It may be helpful for you to determine which of these formats is most evident in the argument.

Prediction

Our firm will maximize its productivity if it invests in enhanced information technology.

The directions for crafting your response include suggesting that you identify any questionable Assumptions that may underlie or support the writer's conclusion. The Assumptions may be stated or implied.

Claims and/or Assumptions

    a)   Employee efficiency insures profitability

    b)   Improved IT software and hardware increase the efficiency of employees who do the majority of their work on computers.

To help you create your analysis of the argument, list alternative explanations for the claims made in the argument. What else may explain the events listed? What claims might someone on the opposite side of the argument make?

Alternative explanations and counterclaims

    a)   Profits accrue when expenses are less than income

b)   Efficiency does not guarantee profitability unless it makes the product less costly to produce

The author of the argument may have omitted some information to make his position appear stronger. What information would help you decide if the argument has validity or what should the writer's audience know in order to make an informed decision?

Additional information needed to better evaluate the argument

a)   What percentage of the employees does their work on computers?

b)   The current productivity rate

c)   What type of work is done on computers?

d)   If sales of advertising are declining

Sample Essay

Companies seem to pull out the efficiency card whenever they need to increase profits. "If our employees were more efficient, we'd have greater profits," they like to say. No matter the product or service one is selling, an attractive bottom line is achieved by having sales greater than expenses. If a product is in great demand, greater efficiency in producing it can help to increase profits. If a product or service is out of favor in the marketplace, producing it more efficiently will not contribute to profits.

Advertising is a highly competitive and creative business. But even the glossiest, most creative and efficiently produced ad has no value to the firm if the client doesn't buy it. The most advanced software and hardware can give a company an edge, depending on what work is accomplished with these tools. The percentage of employees who do most of their work on computers is also a factor. The kinds of work done on computers in an advertising agency might be significant. Contracts between the agency and its clients are drafted using word processing software. Publishing software helps to perfect layouts. Presentation software has replaced easels and story boards to show concepts to the clients and print annotated handouts for the meetings. Researchers will use the Internet to find information on trends and create spreadsheets to analyze the effectiveness of various ads. If this is the bulk of the work in an advertising agency, using the latest software and hardware to produce it will improve the efficiency of the workers and, in a business with tight deadlines, possibly affect the bottom line.of course, the information technology department of the ad agency is promoting its own cause. Decision makers cannot overlook the work that is done on the creative and sales sides of the business. There is no business without the skills of the executives who make their pitches to current and prospective clients. The agency would have no product to pitch without the artistic abilities of its creative talent. These cornerstones of the industry are likely to spend little time using technology.

The reader should want to know why the IT department has chosen this point in time to make its plea for more advanced software and hardware. There may be some concern in the company a out falling revenues, and the IT department believes that increased efficiency on its part can help the company become more profitable. Perhaps it has been a long time since IT equipment has been updated, and the older equipment is no longer working well or enabling them to meet company goals and deadlines. Any company that relies on critical part of its work being done using technology should plan for upgrades on a regular basis. The information technology department may have a valid point here.

Argument Task 34

> *The following appeared in an Excelsior Company memorandum:*
>
> *"The Excelsior Company plans to introduce its own brand of coffee. Since coffee is an expensive food item, and since there are already many established brands of coffee, the best way to gain customers for the Excelsior brand is to do what Superior, the leading coffee company, did when it introduced the newest brand in its line of coffees: conduct a temporary sales promotion that offers free samples, price reductions, and discount coupons for the new brand."*
>
> *Discuss how well reasoned you find this argument. In your discussion be sure to analyze the line of reasoning and the use of evidence in the argument. For example, you may need to consider what questionable Assumptions unlike the thinking and what alternative explanations or counter examples might weaken the conclusion. You can also discuss what sort of evidence would strengthen or refute the argument, what changes in the argument would make it more logically sound, and what, if anything, would help you better evaluate its conclusion.*

Strategies

A good place to start your analysis is by creating a statement that reveals the main idea of the argument. Although the writer is creating an argument, he may ultimately be stating a position, making a recommendation, or making a prediction. It may be helpful for you to determine which of these formats is most evident in the argument.

Argument/ recommendation

In order to gain more customers for its new coffee, Excelsior Company should conduct a sales promotion similar to the one Superior conducted when it introduced its newest me of coffee.

The directions for crafting your response include suggesting that you identify any questionable Assumptions that may underlie or support the writer's conclusion. The Assumptions may be stated or implied.

Claims and/or Assumptions

a) Coffee is an expensive food item

b) There are many established brands of coffee

c) Superior is the leading coffee company

d) Free samples, price reductions, and discount coupons is the most effective way to introduce a new coffee brand

e) Superior's new coffee has remained successful

f) Excelsior is a coffee company

To help you create your analysis of the argument, list alternative explanations for the claims made in the argument. What else may explain the events listed? What claims might someone on the opposite side of the argument make?

Alternative explanations and counter claims

   a)   The price of coffee depends on supply and demand

   b)   Other means of promotion may be more effective

   c)   The cost of the promotion is too expensive

   d)   Excelsior is making coffee in addition to other products it also has on the market

The author of the argument may have omitted some information to make his position appear stronger. What information would help you decide if the argument has validity or what should the writer's audience know in order to make an informed decision?

Additional information needed to better evaluate the argument

   a)   How long ago Superior used the introductory promotion

   b)   How successful Superior's new brand has remained

   c)   Excelsior's other products

   d)   How much it will cost Excelsior to get into the coffee business

   e)   If the demand for coffee is high enough to support a new brand

   f)   What Excelsior hopes to gain by introducing its own coffee brand?

Sample Essay

"The world runs on Dunkin'" tell us that coffee is the fuel that keeps our engines running. Starbucks has made the word "barista" familiar to nearly everyone. One can order a latte, cappuccino, espresso, or regular coffee on virtually every street corner in America. The standard percolator is a thing of the past, having been replaced by the French press, Keurig brewers, and coffee stations built into high-priced new homes. Given the volume and variety of coffee sold in America each day, it would be tempting for a company to add its own brand to the mix. If that company has little or no experience marketing coffee, it would also be tempting to use the tactics that appear to have been successful for another company. Following in Superior's footsteps may seem the safest course.

The argument doesn't reveal what products the Excelsior Company already sells. The reader also doesn't know if Excelsior's sales are flat or in decline, so the company is seeking a shot in the arm and has settled on product that has consistently high sales around the world. Trade magazines always advise businesses to do something that makes them stand out in their particular market. If a jeweler wants to open a store in a town with three already established jewelry stores, he would be well-advised to offer a unique product or service rather than be the fourth-best at what the other stores are already doing. A new business will expend a tremendous amount of time, energy, and money to be in that fourth place. If the new business offers something that the others don't, it is already in first place. Rather than enter an already crowded coffee market, Excelsior Company would be better off to focus on improving the products it already sells or introduce an entirely new product to the market.

The memorandum also recommends using the same promotional tactics that Superior used when introducing its newest brand of coffee. Before doing so, Excelsior should research how successful that introductory promotion was.

How many coupons were redeemed on purchases of Superior's new coffee? Does the new brand continue to sell well? How long ago was the promotion? If Excelsior persists in its desire to create its own coffee brand, the company should conduct some market research to determine what type of promotion is most likely to have successful results today.

If Excelsior Company wants to introduce its own brand of coffee, they will need either a source of beans or ground coffee or a facility in which to roast and grind their own beans. Gearing up to develop and create a unique coffee could be so expensive as to make a financial return possible only after years on the market. Excelsior may be better off sticking to what it knows.

Argument Task 35

> *The following appeared as part of an article on government funding of environmental regulatory agencies:*
>
> *"When scientists finally learn how to create large amounts of copper from other chemical elements, the regulation of copper mining will become unnecessary. For one thing, since the amount of potentially available copper will no longer be limited by the quantity of actual copper deposits, the problem of over-mining will quickly be eliminated altogether. For another, manufacturers will not need to use synthetic copper substitutes, the production of which creates pollutants. Thus, since two problems will be settled—over-mining and pollution—it makes good sense to reduce funding for mining regulation and either save the money or reallocate it where it is needed more."*
>
> *Discuss how well reasoned you find this argument. In your discussion be sure to analyze the line of reasoning and the use of evidence in the argument. For example, you may need to consider what questionable Assumptions unlike the thinking and what alternative explanations or counter examples might weaken the conclusion. You can also discuss what sort of evidence would strengthen or refute the argument, what changes in the argument would make it more logically sound, and what, if anything, would help you better evaluate its conclusion.*

Strategies

A good place to start your analysis is by creating a statement that reveals the main idea of the argument. Although the writer is creating an argument, he may ultimately be stating a position, making a recommendation, or making a prediction. It may be helpful for you to determine which of these formats is most evident in the argument.

Recommendation

Reduce the funding for mining regulation and either save it or reallocate it where it is needed more.

The directions for crafting your response include suggesting that you identify any questionable Assumptions that may underlie or support the writer's conclusion. The Assumptions may be stated or implied.

Claims and Assumptions

    a)   Scientists will be able to create copper from other chemical elements

    b)   Over mining will be eliminated

    c)   The process will be profitable

    d)   Demand for copper will remain high

    e)   Pollution caused by manufacture of synthetic copper will be eliminated

To help you create your analysis of the argument, list alternative explanations for the claims made in the

argument. What else may explain the events listed? What claims might someone on the opposite side of the argument make?

Alternative explanations and/or counter examples

a)   Copper is an element and cannot be created by combining other elements

b)   It is unnecessary to create copper from other elements while a supply of natural copper exists

c)   Mining copper creates pollutants

d)   The demand for copper is declining

e)   The synthesis will be too expensive to be practical

The author of the argument may have omitted some information to make his position appear stronger. What information would help you decide if the argument has validity or what should the writer's audience know in order to make an informed decision?

Additional information needed to better evaluate the argument

a)   Timeline for developing the process

b)   Which elements will be combined to create copper

c)   Cost of the process

d)   If the demand for copper remains high or has declined

Sample Essay

The first hurdle to overcome while analyzing this argument is the ability to suspend the knowledge that elements are primary building blocks and cannot be created by combining other elements. Even taking the argument at face value raises some questions that must be answered before acting on the recommendation to reduce funding for agencies that regulate mining. Those agencies regulate all aspect s of mining, including safety and environmental impact. Some contradictory information in the argument makes this recommendation suspect.

The words "when" and "potentially" should raise a red flag. The timeline for the synthesis of other elements into copper is not specified. Decision makers should inquire whether or not any progress has been made or if it is still a hypothesis. Fabricators who rely on a ready and steady supply of copper cannot fill their orders with potentially available product. Regulatory agencies cannot make decisions about their continued existence based on some future possibility. For the foreseeable future, copper mining will continue in a traditional manner and will need oversight by these agencies.

In addition, regulators should know what elements will be used to create copper. It may be that those elements are rare or difficult to extract from their sources. The process of mining them may be dangerous to the miners and/or the environment. The cost of mining these elements may be prohibitive. If the cost of synthesizing other elements to create copper is far greater than natural copper, demand for the new product will decline. Manufactures who have otherwise relied on copper will seek alternatives, making the discovery useless.

The author cites two problems that will be solved by the new process: over-mining and pollution in the creation of

synthetic copper. The term over-mining implies a surplus. If a surplus of copper exists, there is no need for either the current synthetic or the future product suggested in the argument. There is a finite amount of every element. Eventually, the sources of every metal from copper to platinum will be depleted, including the elements that will be combined to create the new copper. The pollutants generated in creating the synthetic copper currently in existence may be no more harmful than pollutants that may be created in the process touted in the argument. At the very least, pollution will occur from the fossil fuels burned by the mining machinery and the trucks used to transport the raw material to the manufacturing plant.

Regardless of the feasibility of this new method for creating copper, mining of some sort will occur. Reducing the number of agencies may lead to abuses by mining companies as they excavate for the elements needed to create a replacement for synthetic copper. In effect, they authors of this argument have stated a case for creating a different synthetic, and the accompanying problems may remain the same for this process as well

Argument Task 36

> *The following appeared in the editorial section of a monthly business news magazine:*
>
> *"Most companies would agree that as the risk of physical injury occurring on the job increases, the wages paid to employees should also increase. Hence it makes financial sense for employers to make the workplace safer: they could thus reduce their payroll expenses and save money."*
>
> *Discuss how well reasoned you find this argument. In your discussion be sure to analyze the line of reasoning and the use of evidence in the argument. For example, you may need to consider what questionable Assumptions unlike the thinking and what alternative explanations or counter examples might weaken the conclusion. You can also discuss what sort of evidence would strengthen or refute the argument, what changes in the argument would make it more logically sound, and what, if anything, would help you better evaluate its conclusion.*

Strategies

Argument

The directions for crafting your response include suggesting that you identify any questionable assumptions that may underlie or support the writer's conclusion. The assumptions may be stated or implied.

Assumptions

a) Workers in dangerous jobs should be paid higher wages

b) Reducing the risk of injury in the workplace will enable employers to lower wages

c) Workers will accept lower pay for work that is less dangerous

d) Workplace safety is an important contribution to a company's profitability

e) Making the workplace safer is less expensive than paying higher wages

To help you create your analysis of the argument, list alternative explanations for the claims made in the argument. What else may explain the events listed? What claims might someone on the opposite side of the argument make?

Alternative explanations and/or counterexamples

a) Wages may rise based on the availability of qualified workers

b) Profitability is determined by sales minus costs

c) Wages are based on skill and educational level

The author of the argument may have omitted some information to make his position appear stronger. What information would help you decide if the argument has validity or what should the writer's audience know in order to make an informed decision?

Additional information needed to better evaluate the argument

a)   The cost of installing safety measures versus paying higher wages for dangerous jobs

b)   What motivates companies to offer higher wages

After completing these steps, you should have enough material to write your analysis. Remember that you are not creating a position of your own; you are evaluating the strengths and weaknesses of the existing argument. You do not have to include all of the points that you have created in your prewriting. In fact, during the process of drafting your analysis, other ideas may come to mind, and, if they strengthen your analysis, you should include them.

Sample Essay

The author of this argument suggests that because employers make a direct link between the risk of physical injury on a job and the wages paid to an employee, employers will increase wages for dangerous jobs. The basic premise behind this argument is a faulty assumption. The author assumes that because companies believe that a risky job should pay more, these companies actually do pay more. In fact, even though employers believe that increasing wages is a cost-effective way of making the workplace safer; employers will not raise wages due to financial motivations.

The author's main argument is flawed in that it assumes that job safety is a primary factor in determining workers' wages. While it may play a role, the desires to save on labor costs, or attract a special skill or skill level are more likely to have a greater influence on pay rates. A job that is much more dangerous, therefore, may not pay more or only a small amount more. By ignoring other factors that may affect wages, the author provides an incomplete and unconvincing argument that more dangerous jobs pay more.

First, many companies may believe, in a hypothetical situation, that a riskier job should have a higher salary. In practice, however, employers do not actually adjust wages upward for workers in dangerous jobs due to financial motivations. Instead, wages are conventionally determined by the supply and demand for workers. Employers will pay the market rate for wages, setting wages as low as they can while still attracting qualified workers. For example, if the number of available workers is low, employers will increase wages to attract workers. Thus, employers are more apt to adjust wages in response to a tight job market than safety concerns.

A second factor affecting wage levels is the skill level required for the work. Employers are more concerned with whether the employee has the right qualifications than how risky the job is. For example, if there is competition for engineers, the employer will increase wages for engineers to gain an advantage in the job market.

Finally, the costs of offering higher wages to attract workers to more dangerous workplaces may outweigh the benefits. Higher wages may attract workers who are better safety managers to risky job positions. These more prudent employees may indeed contribute to a safer work environment. However, employers may be left with a smaller budget to hire more qualified workers into highly skilled positions. A lack of qualified workers is likely to increase workplace safety issues.

While employers may have an ethical and even a legal duty to take steps to improve workplace safety, they do not have strong financial incentives to increase salaries for riskier jobs. To improve competitiveness, as the aforementioned arguments show, employers will offer the lowest salaries workers will accept to keep labor costs low. The need to attract the right skills in a competitive job market is a stronger driver of wage levels than workplace safety.

Argument Task 37

> *The following appeared in the editorial section of a newspaper in the country of West Cambria:*
>
> *"The practice of officially changing speed limits on the highways—whether by increasing or decreasing them—is a dangerous one. Consider what happened over the past decade whenever neighboring East Cambria changed its speed limits: an average of 3 percent more automobile accidents occurred during the week following the change than had occurred during the week preceding it—even when the speed limit was lowered. This statistic shows that the change in speed limit adversely affected the alertness of drivers."*
>
> *Discuss how well reasoned you find this argument. In your discussion be sure to analyze the line of reasoning and the use of evidence in the argument. For example, you may need to consider what questionable Assumptions unlike the thinking and what alternative explanations or counter examples might weaken the conclusion. You can also discuss what sort of evidence would strengthen or refute the argument, what changes in the argument would make it more logically sound, and what, if anything, would help you better evaluate its conclusion.*

Strategies

Argument

The directions for crafting your response include suggesting that you identify any questionable assumptions that may underlie or support the writer's conclusion. The assumptions may be stated or implied.

Assumptions

a) East Cambrian is in the habit of changing its speed limits regularly

b) Raising or lowering the speed limit causes an increase in highway accidents in East Cambria

c) A three percent increase in accidents is a significant number

d) Changing the speed limit affects drivers' alertness

e) Conditions in West Cambria will mimic those in East Cambria

f) Lack of alertness is the main cause of traffic accidents

To help you create your analysis of the argument, list alternative explanations for the claims made in the argument. What else may explain the events listed? What claims might someone on the opposite side of the argument make?

Alternative explanations and/or counterexamples

a) Other factors, such as weather, may have contributed to a higher number of accidents

b) The nature of the roads - curves or hills - may affect drivers' ability to adjust to new speed limits

c) East Cambria may have more traffic than West Cambria

The author of the argument may have omitted some information to make his position appear stronger. What information would help you decide if the argument has validity or what should the writer's audience know in order to make an informed decision?

Additional information needed to better evaluate the argument

a)   Other factors that may have contributed to a higher number of accidents

b)   Whether the speed limits were raised or lowered

c)   The traffic volume in each part of the country

After completing these steps, you should have enough material to write your analysis. Remember that you are not creating a position of your own; you are evaluating the strengths and weaknesses of the existing argument. You do not have to include all of the points that you have created in your prewriting. In fact, during the process of drafting your analysis, other ideas may come to mind, and, if they strengthen your analysis, you should include them.

Sample Essay

The author of this argument contends that a one-week increase in accidents after a change in speed limit shows that changing speed limits is a dangerous practice. This argument lacks merit because it makes comparisons based on flawed assumptions and incomplete data on automobile accidents in two Australian states.

The primary problem with the author's conclusion is that data on driving accidents was compared between West Cambria and East Cambria for too short a period of time to draw conclusive results. Specifically, an increase in accidents of three percent was observed during a one-week period after the speed limit change. A one-week period is not a sufficient length of time to provide an accurate idea about the impact of a speed limit change. Other factors unrelated to the change in speed limit may have been responsible for an increase in the number of accidents but this important information was not considered.

This short-sightedness overlooks any temporary changes in driving behavior that may have occurred as part of an adjustment period to the new speed limit. For instance, there is no evidence to support the fact that the alertness of the drivers was affected by the change in speed limits, as is assumed by the author. In fact, if the different speed limit played a role in increasing accidents at all, it is probably more likely that this effect was a short-term one caused by the fact that drivers were adjusting to the change. If the numbers of accidents are considered over a longer period of time, it may very well decrease once the drivers become used to the change.

Furthermore, the author ignores differences in the driving environment between East and West Cambria that may affect how drivers react to a change in speed limit. East Cambria may not have properly notified the drivers of the change while West Cambria may have done a better job. East Cambria may have had a different starting speed limit or other factors or conditions that made driving conditions very different from West Cambria.

Finally, the author ignores potential benefits that could result from a change in the speed limit. For instance, while there may have been more accidents, it is important to look at whether those accidents were as serious or as likely to cause injury when drivers are traveling at lower speeds. If there are more accidents but less fatalities then it may still be better to make a change to the speed limit.

In sum, it is not logical to compare driving accidents between the two Australian states without considering the many different factors that could potentially affect the rate of automobile accidents. The author's overreliance on incomplete information and lack of context leads to a weak and faulty comparison, and thus an incorrect conclusion on the effectiveness of the new speed limit.

Argument Task 38

> *The following appeared as part of an article on trends in television:*
>
> *"A recent study of viewers' attitudes toward prime-time television programs shows that many of the programs that were judged by their viewers to be of high quality appeared on (noncommercial) television networks, and that, on commercial television, the most popular shows are typically sponsored by the best-selling products. Thus, it follows that businesses who use commercial television to promote their products will achieve the greatest advertising success by sponsoring only highly rated programs—and, ideally, programs resembling the highly rated noncommercial programs on public channels as much as possible."*
>
> *Discuss how well reasoned you find this argument. In your discussion be sure to analyze the line of reasoning and the use of evidence in the argument. For example, you may need to consider what questionable Assumptions unlike the thinking and what alternative explanations or counter examples might weaken the conclusion. You can also discuss what sort of evidence would strengthen or refute the argument, what changes in the argument would make it more logically sound, and what, if anything, would help you better evaluate its conclusion.*

Strategies

Argument

The directions for crafting your response include suggesting that you identify any questionable assumptions that may underlie or support the writer's conclusion. The assumptions may be stated or implied.

Assumptions

a) Highly regarded programs are the most-watched programs

b) Noncommercial networks air higher quality programs than commercial networks

c) The most popular shows on commercial networks are sponsored by the best-selling products

d) Commercial networks air programs similar to the highly-regarded shows on noncommercial networks

e) Advertisers will be more successful if they sponsor programs that are similar to the highly-regarded programs on noncommercial networks

To help you create your analysis of the argument, list alternative explanations for the claims made in the argument. What else may explain the events listed? What claims might someone on the opposite side of the argument make?

Alternative explanations and/or counterexamples

a) People may not actually watch shows that they rank high in quality

b) Advertisers select television shows based on their popularity rather than perceived quality

The author of the argument may have omitted some information to make his position appear stronger. What information would help you decide if the argument has validity or what should the writer's audience know in order to make an informed decision?

Additional information needed to better evaluate the argument

a) The ratings share of highly rated shows

b) The criteria used by advertisers when selecting shows on which to advertise

After completing these steps, you should have enough material to write your analysis. Remember that you are not creating a position of your own; you are evaluating the strengths and weaknesses of the existing argument. You do not have to include all of the points that you have created in your prewriting. In fact, during the process of drafting your analysis, other ideas may come to mind, and, if they strengthen your analysis, you should include them.

Sample Essay

The author of this argument suggests to companies that they should advertise their products on popular television shows similar to those featured on public or non-commercial channels. However, this advice draws on a number of assumptions that are based on false causal inferences about popular shows. Specifically, the author erroneously assumes that there is a connection between popular shows and high quality shows. The author also makes an erroneous assumption that two different audiences will have the same taste in advertising.

The first assumption that the author makes is that viewers actually watch shows that they rate as high quality shows. A viewer may indicate that a non-commercial television show is high quality but not necessarily watch the show. For example, it is not uncommon for highly rated shows to go off the air due to declining viewership. There is no evidence presented to show that "high-quality" non-commercial programs are actually popular, and thus no evidence to indicate that advertising on these programs would provide any additional benefit to companies.

A second faulty assumption is that the audiences for noncommercial and commercial programs have the same taste. The author assumes that shows that perform well on non-commercial stations will also perform well on commercial stations. However, the audience for these two different types of programming may be very different and those who watch primarily commercial television may not be interested in the types of programs popular on non-commercial channels. For instance, children's educational shows may be highly watched on non-commercial channels but a large majority of the audience viewing commercial programming may have little or no interest in this programming.

Finally, the author makes the assumption that the effectiveness of advertising on popular programs is responsible for a brand's success. The author assumes that popular brands are popular because they advertise on the most widely-watched programs. In reality, it may be that only best-selling brands are able to afford the higher cost of advertising on popular shows. Moreover, brands advertising on the most popular shows may simply do more advertising on a wider variety of shows, and this increase in advertising – rather than the specific advertising on popular shows – may account for the brand's success.

The author's advice to marketers is, therefore, flawed since no direct causal connections are shown between advertising on popular shows and the success of a brand. To earn a higher return on advertising dollars, advertisers should conduct solid market research on factors such as program viewership preferences and numbers.

Argument Task 39

> *The following appeared in an ad for a book titled How to Write a Screenplay for a Movie:*
>
> *"Writers who want to succeed should try to write film screenplays rather than books, since the average film tends to make greater profits than does even a best-selling book. It is true that some books are also made into films. However, our nation's film producers are more likely to produce movies based on original screenplays than to produce films based on books, because in recent years the films that have sold the most tickets have usually been based on original screenplays."*
>
> *Discuss how well reasoned you find this argument. In your discussion be sure to analyze the line of reasoning and the use of evidence in the argument. For example, you may need to consider what questionable Assumptions unlike the thinking and what alternative explanations or counter examples might weaken the conclusion. You can also discuss what sort of evidence would strengthen or refute the argument, what changes in the argument would make it more logically sound, and what, if anything, would help you better evaluate its conclusion.*

Strategies

Argument

The directions for crafting your response include suggesting that you identify any questionable assumptions that may underlie or support the writer's conclusion. The assumptions may be stated or implied.

Assumptions

a) Writers measure success by the amount of money they make

b) Film producers pay large sums for original screenplays

c) The amount of money paid to a writer for a screenplay exceeds the amount of money the authors can make from book sales

d) Ticket sales have an effect on the amount of money paid to the writer of the screenplay

e) A writer is more likely to have an original screenplay made into a move than to have a best-selling book

f) The most successful films will continue to be based on original screenplays rather than book adaptations

To help you create your analysis of the argument, list alternative explanations for the claims made in the argument. What else may explain the events listed? What claims might someone on the opposite side of the argument make?

Alternative explanations and/or counterexamples

a) Writers may write for reasons other than financial success, such as critical acclaim

   b)   Some writers make millions of dollars a year from book sales, a sum that may not be realized from writing an original screenplay

   c)   It is impossible to predict that original screenplays will continue to produce more successful movies than book adaptations

The author of the argument may have omitted some information to make his position appear stronger. What information would help you decide if the argument has validity or what should the writer's audience know in order to make an informed decision?

Additional information needed to better evaluate the argument

   a)   The amount paid for an original screenplay versus the book sales for a best-selling author

   b)   Whether the most successful movies have always been made from original screenplays

After completing these steps, you should have enough material to write your analysis. Remember that you are not creating a position of your own; you are evaluating the strengths and weaknesses of the existing argument. You do not have to include all of the points that you have created in your prewriting. In fact, during the process of drafting your analysis, other ideas may come to mind, and, if they strengthen your analysis, you should include them.

Sample Essay

The author suggests that writers should write screenplays rather than books if they want to find success. Given the current popularity of original screenplays, the author reasons that films make more profits than books, and original screenplays are more likely to be made into films than books are. However, the author makes numerous faulty assumptions about how writers define success and about how producers choose which films to make.

The premise for the argument that writers define success in terms of financial gain is not supported by factual evidence but false assumptions. People may write for many other reasons than achieving financial success. J.K. Rowland, for example, wrote the Harry Potter books because she loved telling stories, yet they ultimately were turned into top grossing movies. Thus, authors may define success as literary merit or audience acceptance rather than making the most amount of money possible.

Nonetheless, the author makes a number of assumptions based on such faulty causality to show that screenplays will lead to financial success. First, the author disregards the fact that an author may be much more likely to write a best-selling book than have an original screenplay made into a movie. Indeed, in the era of self-publishing and Internet marketing, arguably an author has a greater chance of publishing a successful book than having a screenplay made into a movie. Absent supporting evidence, the prospects for success of a screenwriter are based on unsubstantiated information.

Second, the author assumes that film profits go directly to the author of the book. In reality, just because a film is more profitable than a best-selling book does not mean that the writer enjoys these greater profits. Many of the profits may be kept by the actors, movie studios and others involved in the production of the film.

Finally, the author assumes that movie studios are more likely to choose original screenplays than books as the basis of films because in recent years films based on screenplays have enjoyed more success. However, this may have occurred because the original screenplays were simply on more interesting topics or captured the attention of filmgoers. In the future, books may be equally likely to be interesting or attention getting and movie studios will likely judge both books and original screenplays based on their merit.

Writers, therefore, should avoid choosing to write screenplays over books based on these unsupported assumptions. To make more informed decisions, authors should rely on concrete research on book publishing and screenwriting industry trends.

Argument Task 40

> *The following appeared in a memorandum from the ElectroWares Company's marketing department:*
>
> *"Since our company started manufacturing and marketing a deluxe light bulb six months ago, sales of our economy light bulb—and company profits—have decreased significantly. Although the deluxe light bulb sells for 50 percent more than the economy bulb, it lasts twice as long. Therefore, to increase repeat sales and maximize profits, we should discontinue the deluxe light bulb."*
>
> *Discuss how well reasoned you find this argument. In your discussion be sure to analyze the line of reasoning and the use of evidence in the argument. For example, you may need to consider what questionable Assumptions unlike the thinking and what alternative explanations or counter examples might weaken the conclusion. You can also discuss what sort of evidence would strengthen or refute the argument, what changes in the argument would make it more logically sound, and what, if anything, would help you better evaluate its conclusion.*

Strategies

Argument

The directions for crafting your response include suggesting that you identify any questionable assumptions that may underlie or support the writer's conclusion. The assumptions may be stated or implied.

Assumptions

   a) Declining sales of economy light bulbs has adversely affected company profits

   b) Discontinuing sales of deluxe light bulbs will maximize profits

   c) Other economic factors have no effect on the company profits

   d) Prior to introducing the deluxe light bulb, the company made satisfactory profits

To help you create your analysis of the argument, list alternative explanations for the claims made in the argument. What else may explain the events listed? What claims might someone on the opposite side of the argument make?

Alternative explanations and/or counterexamples

   a) Other expenses may account for the decline in profits

   b) Other companies have also introduced a deluxe lightbulb increasing competition for sales

The author of the argument may have omitted some information to make his position appear stronger. What information would help you decide if the argument has validity or what should the writer's audience know in order to make an informed decision?

Additional information needed to better evaluate the argument

a) Has there been an increase in wages or other overhead expenses?

b) Have other companies recently introduced a similar lightbulb?

After completing these steps, you should have enough material to write your analysis. Remember that you are not creating a position of your own; you are evaluating the strengths and weaknesses of the existing argument. You do not have to include all of the points that you have created in your prewriting. In fact, during the process of drafting your analysis, other ideas may come to mind, and, if they strengthen your analysis, you should include them.

Sample Essay

The author assumes that the deluxe light bulb and its longer lifespan are responsible for the company's reduced profits. While the drop in profits did indeed coincide with the introduction of the deluxe light bulb, no concrete evidence is provided to show that the new product was the cause of the decline. The conclusion to discontinue the deluxe light bulb, therefore, is based on unfounded assumptions instead of product and market research.

The major premise that the manufacturing and marketing of the deluxe light bulb is the cause of a decline in economy light bulb sales and thus the company's profits is based on false reasoning. The fact that the introduction of the deluxe light bulb coincided with the reduction in profits does not necessarily mean that it was the cause of the reduction. The timing may have been coincidental. The reduction in profits may have occurred due to other factors such as a shift in consumer preferences, or increased marketing and manufacturing costs.

If other factors are indeed responsible for the reduction in profits, the assumption that discontinuing the deluxe bulb will result in the company's profits returning is also flawed. For example, consumers may have switched from economy light bulbs or competitors may be offering deluxe bulbs at a lower price. If there were other reasons for the reduction in profit, discontinuing the deluxe bulb could have no effect on profits. Worse, the company would end up losing the money that it spent on marketing and manufacturing if it is not able to sell the deluxe bulb.

Equally flawed is the argument that the company should discontinue the deluxe bulb because it lasts longer. It fails to recognize that people are already paying more for the longer-lasting technology and may be willing to pay twice as much for a bulb that lasts twice as long. Perhaps a better solution, then, would be to increase the price of the deluxe bulb, especially since the company has already spent money on marketing and manufacturing.

Because the author's argument is based on flawed assumptions, about the cause of the sales decline the company is given ill-conceived advice on how best to proceed. The company should conduct more market and product research to discover the real reason for the reduction in profits in recent months. It can then re-evaluate its options and create a more viable strategy for improving profitability.

Argument Task 41

> *The following appeared as part of an article in a local newspaper:*
>
> *"Over the past three years the tartfish industry has changed markedly: fishing technology has improved significantly, and the demand for tartfish has grown in both domestic and foreign markets. As this trend continues, the tartfish industry on Shrimp Island can expect to experience the same overfishing problems that are already occurring with mainland fishing industries: without restrictions on fishing, fishers see no reason to limit their individual catches. As the catches get bigger, the tartfish population will be dangerously depleted while the surplus of tartfish will devalue the catch for fishers. Government regulation is the only answer: tartfish-fishing should be allowed only during the three-month summer season, when tartfish reproduce and thus are most numerous, rather than throughout the year."*
>
> *Discuss how well reasoned you find this argument. In your discussion be sure to analyze the line of reasoning and the use of evidence in the argument. For example, you may need to consider what questionable Assumptions unlike the thinking and what alternative explanations or counter examples might weaken the conclusion. You can also discuss what sort of evidence would strengthen or refute the argument, what changes in the argument would make it more logically sound, and what, if anything, would help you better evaluate its conclusion.*

Strategies

Argument

The directions for crafting your response include suggesting that you identify any questionable assumptions that may underlie or support the writer's conclusion. The assumptions may be stated or implied.

Assumptions

a)   Tartfish fishermen fail to recognize the importance of maintaining the fish population

b)   The demand for Tartfish will continue to expand

c)   Fishing only during the season when Tartfish reproduce will preserve the fish population

d)   There are no regulations on mainland fishing

e)   Lack of regulation contributed to overfishing on the mainland

To help you create your analysis of the argument, list alternative explanations for the claims made in the argument. What else may explain the events listed? What claims might someone on the opposite side of the argument make?

Alternative explanations and/or counterexamples

a)   The demand for Tartfish will not exceed the supply

b) The populations of other fish may have declined for reasons other than overfishing

c) Fishing only during the reproductive cycle may have a negative effect on the next year's supply of Tartfish

The author of the argument may have omitted some information to make his position appear stronger. What information would help you decide if the argument has validity or what should the writer's audience know in order to make an informed decision?

Additional information needed to better evaluate the argument

a) Why overfishing has occurred with mainland species

b) The rate of increase in demand for Tartfish

After completing these steps, you should have enough material to write your analysis. Remember that you are not creating a position of your own; you are evaluating the strengths and weaknesses of the existing argument. You do not have to include all of the points that you have created in your prewriting. In fact, during the process of drafting your analysis, other ideas may come to mind, and, if they strengthen your analysis, you should include them.

Sample Essay

The author argues that tartfish will be overfished similar to other mainland fishing industries because the demand for tartfish has grown and technologies have advanced. However, the assumption that the conditions leading to overfishing in one industry apply to the tartfish industry is drawn from a weak analogy. Therefore, the proposed solution of government regulation of tartfish fishing is also weak since it is based on false assumptions.

The very premise of the argument is weak because it is based on a comparison of fishing industries that may not be alike in important aspects. The author assumes that the tartfish industry will experience overfishing problems simply because other fishing industries have. However, every industry is different and the demand for tartfish may not necessarily exceed the supply of tartfish. There is no solid evidence presented to indicate that what has happened in other industries will also happen with tartfish. Given the lack of evidence from the fishing industry, the author's argument cannot be trusted.

The author further assumes that the fishermen in the tartfish industry can only be stopped from overfishing by government regulation. This ignores the possibility that the fishermen may have other motivations for avoiding overfishing, such as a respect for the environment or a desire to ensure their continued livelihood by protecting the tartfish population.

Finally, even if the author is correct in concluding that government regulation is necessary, the proposed fishing season could lead to an even greater shortage. It is assumed that allowing fishing only during the reproductive season would be best because the supply of tartfish is greatest at this time. However, if the fish are caught during their reproductive season, then the reproductive process is likely to be interrupted, resulting in fewer tartfish the following year. The regulation would thus have the opposite effect than what was intended.

The development of a fishing policy for tartfish should be based on sound industry research. Proceeding with an overfishing policy based on false assumptions could create economic problems for the tartfish industry. Therefore, it would be unwise for the tartfish industry to follow the author's call for regulation without first conducting more research into the factors affecting supply and demand in the tartfish industry.

Argument Task 42

> *The following appeared in the editorial section of a local paper:*
>
> *"Applications for advertising spots on KMTV, our local cable television channel, decreased last year. Meanwhile a neighboring town's local channel, KOOP, changed its focus to farming issues and reported an increase in advertising applications for the year. To increase applications for its advertisement spots, KMTV should focus its programming on farming issues as well."*
>
> *Discuss how well reasoned you find this argument. In your discussion be sure to analyze the line of reasoning and the use of evidence in the argument. For example, you may need to consider what questionable Assumptions unlike the thinking and what alternative explanations or counter examples might weaken the conclusion. You can also discuss what sort of evidence would strengthen or refute the argument, what changes in the argument would make it more logically sound, and what, if anything, would help you better evaluate its conclusion.*

Strategies

Argument

The directions for crafting your response include suggesting that you identify any questionable assumptions that may underlie or support the writer's conclusion. The assumptions may be stated or implied.

Assumptions

   a)   KOOP's changing its focus to farming issues accounts for its increase in advertising applications

   b)   KMTV's reduction in applications for advertising is caused by the station's programming focus

   c)   KMTV and KOOP charge the same amount for advertising spots

   d)   KMTV and KOOP have the same number of advertising minutes in their inventories

   e)   KMTV's advertising applications will increase if it's changes its focus to farming issues

   f)   Farming issues are the most important topic to people in this geographic area

To help you create your analysis of the argument, list alternative explanations for the claims made in the argument. What else may explain the events listed? What claims might someone on the opposite side of the argument make?

Alternative explanations and/or counterexamples

   a)   Farming topics are not as important for KMTV's viewers

   b)   The increase in advertising resulted from other factors, for example, holiday promotions

   c)   KMTV may already have all the advertisers it needs to fill its spots

The author of the argument may have omitted some information to make his position appear stronger. What

information would help you decide if the argument has validity or what should the writer's audience know in order to make an informed decision?

Additional information needed to better evaluate the argument

a) If KMTV has experienced a decline in advertising revenues

b) If KMTV viewers have asked for more programming about farm issues

c) The cost of advertising spots on each station

After completing these steps, you should have enough material to write your analysis. Remember that you are not creating a position of your own; you are evaluating the strengths and weaknesses of the existing argument. You do not have to include all of the points that you have created in your prewriting. In fact, during the process of drafting your analysis, other ideas may come to mind, and, if they strengthen your analysis, you should include them.

Sample Essay

The author suggests that because KOOP experienced an increase in advertising applications after changing its focus to farming, KMTV should also change its focus to farming in order to increase applications for advertising. In making this argument, the author incorrectly assumes that the results KOOP experienced would be the same for KMTV, and thus KMTV will also benefit from a change to farming. However, the author fails to support these assumptions with logical reasoning.

The premise of the author's argument is based on a weak comparison of the programming strategies of two TV stations in different cities. The assumption that advertising results at KOOP will be the same at KMTV is illogical since the towns likely differ in important aspects. For example, they may have different demographics and TV viewership patterns. If KMTV is not a farming town, then a program on farming similar to KOOP's is unlikely to result in an increase in viewership, and thus advertising at KMTV. No evidence is provided to show that the two stations share similar audience demographics.

Even if the TV stations share similar viewership profiles, the author applies false causality to support a farming strategy at KMTV. First, the author assumes that a switch to farming was the cause of the increased number of ad applications at KOOP. In fact, the increase in applications may have occurred for a variety of reasons. For example, it may have been the result of a change in advertising rates under the new station, or it may simply have resulted from the fact that a new programming format appealed to new advertisers. Moreover, once the farming program has been in place for more than a year, the number of advertisers who wish to submit ads is likely to decrease because those who want ads will already have them.

More significantly, the assumption that KMTV has a programming problem at all is not substantiated. KMTV may be experiencing a reduction in ad applications not because its current programming format is not working, but instead because it already has an advertising relationship in place with all potential advertisers. If it switches its programming format and once again develops relationships with all potential advertisers, the number of applications will eventually decrease again. To increase advertising revenues, KMTV will have to increase the value of the ad slots.

To increase the value of advertising, it is important to ensure the programming reflects the interests of the TV station's market. Developing a programming strategy based on faulty assumptions and comparisons between the two TV markets could result in an even larger advertising decline at KMTV. The radio station would need to uncover the reason for its reduction in advertising applications and gain a better understanding of its demographics before proceeding with determining how to increase the number of applications.

Argument Task 43

> The following appeared in a letter to prospective students from the admissions office at Plateau College:
>
> "Every person who earned an advanced degree in science or engineering from Olympus University last year received numerous offers of excellent jobs. Typically, many graduates of Plateau College have gone on to pursue advanced degrees at Olympus. Therefore, enrolling as an undergraduate at Plateau College is a wise choice for students who wish to ensure success in their careers."
>
> Discuss how well reasoned you find this argument. In your discussion be sure to analyze the line of reasoning and the use of evidence in the argument. For example, you may need to consider what questionable Assumptions unlike the thinking and what alternative explanations or counter examples might weaken the conclusion. You can also discuss what sort of evidence would strengthen or refute the argument, what changes in the argument would make it more logically sound, and what, if anything, would help you better evaluate its conclusion.

Strategies

Argument

The directions for crafting your response include suggesting that you identify any questionable assumptions that may underlie or support the writer's conclusion. The assumptions may be stated or implied.

Assumptions

   a) All graduates of Olympus University are as successful as those with science or engineering degrees

   b) A degree from Plateau College is the gateway to attending Olympus University

   c) The possibility of attending Olympus University is an incentive to apply to Plateau College

   d) The number of those earnings advanced degrees in science or engineering from Olympus University is large enough to be statistically significant in the labor market

   e) Applicants with advanced degrees in science or engineering from other schools are not as successful as those from Olympus University

   f) A significant number of graduates of Plateau College attend Olympus University to earn an advanced degree

To help you create your analysis of the argument, list alternative explanations for the claims made in the argument. What else may explain the events listed? What claims might someone on the opposite side of the argument make?

Alternative explanations and/or counterexamples

   a) The demand for graduates with degrees in science or engineering may decline

b)   Graduates with science or engineering degrees from any school quickly find employment

c)   Competition for acceptance at Olympus may prevent students from Plateau's being accepted at the same rate in future years

d)   Graduates of Plateau experience equal success at other graduate schools

The author of the argument may have omitted some information to make his position appear stronger. What information would help you decide if the argument has validity or what should the writer's audience know in order to make an informed decision?

Additional information needed to better evaluate the argument

a)   The current demand for graduates with science or engineering degrees

b)   If graduates of Olympus have more success in the job market than graduates with similar degrees from other schools

After completing these steps, you should have enough material to write your analysis. Remember that you are not creating a position of your own; you are evaluating the strengths and weaknesses of the existing argument. You do not have to include all of the points that you have created in your prewriting. In fact, during the process of drafting your analysis, other ideas may come to mind, and, if they strengthen your analysis, you should include them.

Sample Essay

The author of this argument suggests that students should attend the Plateau undergraduate college because students from that university typically go on to graduate school at Olympus, a college whose graduates in science and engineering receive many good job offers. The assumption, however, that student academic performance, student choice of a major, and job markets will remain the same has led to a misleading conclusion about the job prospects of future Plateau graduates.

First, the author assumes that future students will receive the same job offers as past students provided they graduate from the same school, Olympus, with the same major. There are numerous problems with this assumption. For instance, it ignores the fact that the job market can change and that demand for people within a particular profession can fluctuate. There may be fewer jobs in the same field by the time future students' graduate.

Second, the author ignores the fact that past students may have been smarter, earned better grades or otherwise had better credentials that led to their job offers. Other schools may compete more aggressively for the best students. As a result, future Olympus students may not have the characteristics that were most attractive to employers.

Third, the author assumes that the good job offers occurred because the students earned degrees from Olympus University. In fact, high demand for science and engineering graduates may have been the real driver. It is equally possible that students with science and engineering degrees from any school would also have received lucrative job offers.

The author further ignores the potential for changes in the job and higher education markets. The author incorrectly assumes that Olympus will continue to accept students from Plateau at the same rate as in the past, that Plateau students will continue to want to attend Plateau and that these students will decide to pursue degrees in science and engineering. Students may attend Plateau but be unable to get into Olympus or may get into Olympus but study a different field. Under these scenarios, the author's conditions supporting job market success are no longer valid.

Finally, the author suggests that students who receive numerous job offers will enjoy success in their careers. This, too, is a faulty assumption as these students could get a good job but be fired a short time later or may decide to switch to a different career field. Since it is impossible to show that offers of a good job will always lead to future career success, the entire premise behind the author's argument is flawed.

Argument Task 44

> The following appeared in an editorial from a newspaper serving the town of Saluda:
>
> "The Saluda Consolidated High School offers more than 200 different courses from which its students can choose. A much smaller private school down the street offers a basic curriculum of only 80 different courses, but it consistently sends a higher proportion of its graduating seniors on to college than Consolidated does. By eliminating at least half of the courses offered there and focusing on a basic curriculum, we could improve student performance at Consolidated and also save many tax dollars."
>
> Discuss how well reasoned you find this argument. In your discussion be sure to analyze the line of reasoning and the use of evidence in the argument. For example, you may need to consider what questionable Assumptions unlike the thinking and what alternative explanations or counter examples might weaken the conclusion. You can also discuss what sort of evidence would strengthen or refute the argument, what changes in the argument would make it more logically sound, and what, if anything, would help you better evaluate its conclusion.

Strategies

Argument

The directions for crafting your response include suggesting that you identify any questionable assumptions that may underlie or support the writer's conclusion. The assumptions may be stated or implied.

Assumptions

a) Students at Consolidated and the private school have the same academic abilities

b) A basic curriculum ensures more academic success

c) Offering fewer courses would provide a tax savings for the citizens of Saluda

d) Saluda can meet the needs of its students with fewer course offerings

e) The number of students from the private school who enter college is significantly higher than the number from Saluda who go on to college

To help you create your analysis of the argument, list alternative explanations for the claims made in the argument. What else may explain the events listed? What claims might someone on the opposite side of the argument make?

Alternative explanations and/or counterexamples

a) Academic success depends on the rigor of courses rather than the number of courses offered

b) Saluda Consolidated has a less homogeneous student body than the private school, requiring them to offer a wider variety of courses

c) Offering fewer courses doesn't reduce the need for the same number of teachers, thereby failing to reduce costs for Saluda

Additional information needed to better evaluate the argument

a) The actual percentage of graduates from each high school that go on to college

b) The rigor of the courses offered at each school

After completing these steps, you should have enough material to write your analysis. Remember that you are not creating a position of your own; you are evaluating the strengths and weaknesses of the existing argument. You do not have to include all of the points that you have created in your prewriting. In fact, during the process of drafting your analysis, other ideas may come to mind, and, if they strengthen your analysis, you should include them.

Sample Essay

In evaluating the best school curriculum, the author suggests that a public school should offer fewer courses similar to a local private school that sends more students to college. Unfortunately, the author's arguments are based on faulty causality, and therefore provide weak support for a curriculum with fewer courses.

The first major problem with the author's argument is that it is based on the assumption that the private school sends more students to college because it has fewer courses. In fact, it is unlikely that the reduced number of courses is alone responsible for the private school's higher rate of college attendance. Instead, the private school may have more rigorous academic programs, more involved parents, stricter admissions standards, better teachers or other characteristics that make its students more likely to attend college.

Second, based on the author's faulty assumption that private school students choosing from fewer courses are more likely to attend college, it is further concluded that the fewer courses contribute to higher academic achievement. The reasoning is that the school will be more focused on the basic curriculum if there are fewer courses offered and thus students will perform better. However, this may contradict evidence that student performance and motivation are correlated with the level of personal interest in a subject. Instead of improving their performance or desire to attend college simply because they have fewer class choices, the opposite may occur. Students may perform worse academically because the classes that most interest them may no longer be offered.

Finally, the author assumes it would cost less to provide fewer course offerings. This is likely untrue as well. The same number of students would need to be educated, so teachers would still need to be employed to provide them with instruction. The school would need more teachers that teach general curriculum courses instead of teachers that teach specialized courses. The cost would likely not be reduced, and there is no reason to believe the quality of the education would be improved.

By identifying a causal relationship between the number of courses and the number of students attending college when there is no evidence of any such relationship, the author has drawn an incorrect conclusion. More information is required on the factors influencing college attendance, higher achievement and the quality of education. There is, therefore, no reason to assume that reducing the number of course offerings would improve student performance.

Argument Task 45

> *The following appeared as part of an article in the book section of a newspaper:*
>
> *"Currently more and more books are becoming available in electronic form—either free-of-charge on the Internet or for a very low price-per-book on compact disc.* Thus literary classics are likely to be read more widely than ever before. People who couldn't have purchased these works at bookstore prices will now be able to read them for little or no money; similarly, people who find it inconvenient to visit libraries and wait for books to be returned by other patrons will now have access to whatever classic they choose from their home or work computers. This increase in access to literary classics will radically affect the public taste in reading, creating a far more sophisticated and learned reading audience than has ever existed before.*
>
> **A compact disc is a small portable disc capable of storing relatively large amounts of data that can be read by a computer.*
>
> *Discuss how well reasoned you find this argument. In your discussion be sure to analyze the line of reasoning and the use of evidence in the argument. For example, you may need to consider what questionable Assumptions unlike the thinking and what alternative explanations or counter examples might weaken the conclusion. You can also discuss what sort of evidence would strengthen or refute the argument, what changes in the argument would make it more logically sound, and what, if anything, would help you better evaluate its conclusion.*

Strategies

Argument

The directions for crafting your response include suggesting that you identify any questionable assumptions that may underlie or support the writer's conclusion. The assumptions may be stated or implied.

Assumptions

a)   People have not read literary classics because they are too expensive, or it is inconvenient to visit a library

b)   A large number of people read books in electronic format

c)   Literary classics are frequently checked out at libraries

d)   Greater availability of literary classics will increase the number of people reading them

e)   Reading books other than literary classics is a display of bad taste

f)   The current reading audience is neither sophisticated nor learned

To help you create your analysis of the argument, list alternative explanations for the claims made in the argument. What else may explain the events listed? What claims might someone on the opposite side of the argument make?

Alternative explanations and/or counterexamples

a) People do not read the classics because they are too difficult or uninteresting

b) No matter the format, people will continue to read the types of books they have always read

c) Reading fiction of any type is not likely to make one more learned

The author of the argument may have omitted some information to make his position appear stronger. What information would help you decide if the argument has validity or what should the writer's audience know in order to make an informed decision?

Additional information needed to better evaluate the argument

a) If literary classics have become more popular with the advent of electronic access to them

b) Whether the purchase price of classics in bookstores is higher than that of other types of novels

After completing these steps, you should have enough material to write your analysis. Remember that you are not creating a position of your own; you are evaluating the strengths and weaknesses of the existing argument. You do not have to include all of the points that you have created in your prewriting. In fact, during the process of drafting your analysis, other ideas may come to mind, and, if they strengthen your analysis, you should include them.

Sample Essay

The author argues that easy access to literary classics made possible by new technologies will encourage more people to read classics which will, in turn, make people more educated. Unfortunately, the author makes many faulty assumptions about the role of access, cost and convenience in book choice that raises questions about the veracity of his conclusion.

The first and most fundamental assumption that underlies the author's argument is that people do not read the classics because they do not have easy access to them or because they do not want to pay for them. This ignores the fact that many people simply prefer other reading material or find the classics boring, outdated or too difficult to read for pleasure. The introduction of ebook readers such as Kindle, for example, has increased the number of readers but the types of books on best seller lists have remained the same.

A second related assumption is that people choose their reading material simply based on what is convenient to access and low-cost. In fact, there is no evidence to suggest that reading habits will change with the method of delivery. The earlier transition to compact discs provides a good analogy. Many other books besides the classics were made available on compact discs and readers were just as likely to access those books as they were the classics. Thus, past experience shows that readers may be more apt to simply use the technology to gain easier access to the same type of material they already read.

Even if the author is correct and more people do read classic literature because of new technologies, the author does not provide proof that this will actually lead to people becoming more sophisticated or educated. While reading can expand one's mind, nonfiction is more likely to be educational than works of fiction such as the classics. Moreover, people might read this literature and find that they do not enjoy it, or they may not understand some works such as Shakespeare without guidance, and thus would not become any more sophisticated or learned at all.

Considering the many assumptions made by the author, it is clear that there is no solid evidence to support the theory that Internet books will result in a smarter or more literary audience of classic lovers. As demonstrated above, technology may create access, cost and convenience advantages that affect the format and frequency of book delivery but not the choice of content.

Argument Task 46

> *The following appeared as part of a business plan created by the management of the Take Heart Fitness Center:*
>
> *"After opening the new swimming pool early last summer, Take Heart saw a 12 percent increase in the use of the center by its members. Therefore, in order to increase membership in Take Heart, we should continue to add new recreational facilities in subsequent years: for example, a multipurpose game room, a tennis court, and a miniature golf course. Being the only center in the area offering this range of activities would give us a competitive advantage in the health and recreation market."*
>
> *Discuss how well reasoned you find this argument. In your discussion be sure to analyze the line of reasoning and the use of evidence in the argument. For example, you may need to consider what questionable Assumptions unlike the thinking and what alternative explanations or counter examples might weaken the conclusion. You can also discuss what sort of evidence would strengthen or refute the argument, what changes in the argument would make it more logically sound, and what, if anything, would help you better evaluate its conclusion.*

Strategies

Argument

The directions for crafting your response include suggesting that you identify any questionable assumptions that may underlie or support the writer's conclusion. The assumptions may be stated or implied.

Assumptions

   a) A new swimming pool has caused a 12 percent increase in the use of Take Heart's center

   b) Additional facilities will create a further increase in use of the center

   c) The pool will continue to be responsible for an increase in center use

   d) A wider variety of activities will give Take Heart a competitive edge in the healthy and recreation market

To help you create your analysis of the argument, list alternative explanations for the claims made in the argument. What else may explain the events listed? What claims might someone on the opposite side of the argument make?

Alternative explanations and/or counterexamples

   a) The weather may have caused an increase in the use of Take Heart's facility

   b) Greater use of the facility by current members does not necessarily lead to new members joining

   c) There may already be a variety of facilities available in the area

d)   Adding more facilities may increase membership costs and lead to a decline in membership

The author of the argument may have omitted some information to make his position appear stronger. What information would help you decide if the argument has validity or what should the writer's audience know in order to make an informed decision?

Additional information needed to better evaluate the argument

a)   What other recreational facilities exist in the area

b)   What other factors affected the increase in usage of Take Heart's facility

c)   The reasons for Take Heart's members joining that facility

After completing these steps, you should have enough material to write your analysis. Remember that you are not creating a position of your own; you are evaluating the strengths and weaknesses of the existing argument. You do not have to include all of the points that you have created in your prewriting. In fact, during the process of drafting your analysis, other ideas may come to mind, and, if they strengthen your analysis, you should include them.

Sample Essay

The author argues that a recreation center can increase its competitive advantage and attract new members by expanding its recreational offerings. The basis of this argument is the assumption that the opening of a new swimming pool led to an increase in the use of the recreation center by members. Unfortunately, this underlying assumption is incorrect and supported by faulty causalities.

The basic premise upon which all assumptions are developed is that the addition of the swimming pool was the cause of the increase in use of the recreation center. While this might seem like a logical assumption, the author would need to support this statement with further facts since causation cannot necessarily be assumed simply because one thing happens after another. For example, higher summer temperatures than normal would lead to an increase in users of swimming pools.

Even if the swimming pool addition did increase member use of the facilities, this does not provide support for the author's argument that the center can increase its membership numbers by adding different recreational facilities. This reasoning is based on several faulty assumptions. First, just because more people who are already members increase their use of the facilities due to a new recreational addition does not mean that more people will join who are not already members. Other recreational facilities, for example, could also be adding new programs and increasing the competition for new members. The author presents no evidence that the number of new members rose as a result of the pool.

Second, the author assumes that other recreational facilities such as tennis courts would have the same impact as a swimming pool, which is not necessarily the case. Again, the author fails to consider market competition. For example, a large number of free tennis courts in the area or low-cost lessons at other recreation centers could decrease demand for new tennis facilities.

Finally, the author does not present any solid evidence to show that the number of activities a location has is important to current or potential members. People may be motivated by many factors when joining a recreational facility, including proximity to their location, cost, and whether the facility has a specific activity they enjoy.

If the club expands its recreational activities based on arguments formed by weak causalities, it may spend a great deal of money adding new facilities without any solid evidence that it will recover its costs, gain an advantage over competitors or attract new members. The author's argument, therefore, should not be considered valid unless there is more conclusive proof that these factors will positively affect recreational facility attendance.

Argument Task 47

The following appeared as part of a letter to the editor of a local newspaper:

"Bayview High School is considering whether to require all of its students to wear uniforms while at school. Students attending Acorn Valley Academy, a private school in town, earn higher grades on average and are more likely to go on to college. Moreover, Acorn Valley reports few instances of tardiness, absenteeism, or discipline problems. Since Acorn Valley requires its students to wear uniforms, Bayview High School would do well to follow suit and require its students to wear uniforms as well."

Discuss how well reasoned you find this argument. In your discussion be sure to analyze the line of reasoning and the use of evidence in the argument. For example, you may need to consider what questionable Assumptions unlike the thinking and what alternative explanations or counter examples might weaken the conclusion. You can also discuss what sort of evidence would strengthen or refute the argument, what changes in the argument would make it more logically sound, and what, if anything, would help you better evaluate its conclusion.

Strategies

Argument

The directions for crafting your response include suggesting that you identify any questionable assumptions that may underlie or support the writer's conclusion. The assumptions may be stated or implied.

Assumptions

a) Wearing uniforms will cause Bayview students to earn higher grades

b) More students from Bayview High School will go to college if they switch to uniforms

c) Wearing uniforms ensures that students at Acorn Valley avoid tardiness, absenteeism, and discipline problems

d) If students at Bayview wear uniforms, their behavior will mimic that of students at Acorn Valley

e) Switching to uniforms will have only positive results at Bayview

To help you create your analysis of the argument, list alternative explanations for the claims made in the argument. What else may explain the events listed? What claims might someone on the opposite side of the argument make?

Alternative explanations and/or counterexamples

a) Acorn Valley may have more serious consequences for tardiness, absenteeism, and misbehavior

b) More parents of Acorn Valley students are college graduates than parents of students at Bayview High School

c)   Discipline policies at Bayview High School are inconsistently enforced

d)   Acorn Valley accepts only high achieving students

The author of the argument may have omitted some information to make his position appear stronger. What information would help you decide if the argument has validity or what should the writer's audience know in order to make an informed decision?

Additional information needed to better evaluate the argument

a)   How uniforms affect behavior and academic success in several schools

b)   Discipline procedures at both schools

c)   The education level of parents of students at both schools

After completing these steps, you should have enough material to write your analysis. Remember that you are not creating a position of your own; you are evaluating the strengths and weaknesses of the existing argument. You do not have to include all of the points that you have created in your prewriting. In fact, during the process of drafting your analysis, other ideas may come to mind, and, if they strengthen your analysis, you should include them.

Sample Essay

The author suggests that Bayview High School should require all students to wear uniforms since Acorn Valley Academy requires uniforms and its students have higher grades, fewer disciplinary problems, better attendance and a higher rate of college attendance. Unfortunately, the author's argument is based on a comparison of a private and public school that likely have very different cultures and norms.

First, the primary assumption that the author makes is that the uniform requirement has some impact on attendance, grades, tardiness, college attendance and disciplinary problems. This assumption, which forms the basis for the author's argument, is not supported by any evidence showing a relationship between school uniforms, and better academic performance or more studious behavior. The private school students may have better grades, behavior, and attendance for many reasons unrelated to wearing uniforms. For example, they may be higher achievers because their parents have more resources to send them to college or place more importance on education.

Second, the school with uniforms may have a better reputation or stricter disciplinary policy. Higher performing students will choose to enroll in a school with a good reputation. A well-respected school will also attract the best teachers. To discourage poor academic performance, the school may implement stricter rules, punishments and behavioral strategies, such as limiting access to extracurricular activities and other privileges. More demanding parents will naturally choose an academic program known for its discipline and rigor.

Finally, even if assuming uniforms do have a positive influence on student performance and behavior, the author further weakens his argument by failing to consider differences among schools and students. Among schools that have a uniform requirement, academic performance varies greatly, and thus the experience at Acorn Valley may not be representative of what will happen at Bayview.

Furthermore, the author assumes that students at Bayview High School will react in the same way to a uniform requirement as students at Acorn Valley. There is no evidence to support this relationship. In fact, factors such as differences in socioeconomic backgrounds and experience wearing school uniforms are likely to produce different student behavior.

Because the author incorrectly draws a number of causal relationships between the uniform requirement and the behavior of Acorn Valley students, the author's argument falls apart when these assumptions are challenged. No evidence is produced to show that requiring Bayview High School students to wear uniforms will have any beneficial effect on student performance.

Argument Task 48

> The following appeared in a memorandum written by the assistant manager of a store that sells gourmet food items from various countries:
>
> "A local wine store made an interesting discovery last month: it sold more French than Italian wine on days when it played recordings of French accordion music, but it sold more Italian than French wine on days when Italian songs were played. Therefore, I recommend that we put food specialties from one particular country on sale for a week at a time and play only music from that country while the sale is going on. By this means we will increase our profits in the same way that the wine store did, and we will be able to predict more precisely what items we should stock at any given time."
>
> Discuss how well reasoned you find this argument. In your discussion be sure to analyze the line of reasoning and the use of evidence in the argument. For example, you may need to consider what questionable Assumptions unlike the thinking and what alternative explanations or counter examples might weaken the conclusion. You can also discuss what sort of evidence would strengthen or refute the argument, what changes in the argument would make it more logically sound, and what, if anything, would help you better evaluate its conclusion.

Strategies

Argument

The directions for crafting your response include suggesting that you identify any questionable assumptions that may underlie or support the writer's conclusion. The assumptions may be stated or implied.

Assumptions

   a) Playing a country's music increased the sales of wine produced in that country

   b) Playing a country's music will increase the sales of food from that country

   c) An increase in sales from one country will contribute to greater sales overall

   d) Increasing sales of food from one country will reduce the sales of food from other countries

   e) Increasing sales of food from one country will increase profits

   f) Focusing on one country's food each week will make ordering inventory more efficient

To help you create your analysis of the argument, list alternative explanations for the claims made in the argument. What else may explain the events listed? What claims might someone on the opposite side of the argument make?

Alternative explanations and/or counterexamples

   a) French wines may have been on sale at the same time that the store was playing French music

b) Customers may respond to sales on food in a different manner than sales on wine

c) Increased sales of food from a particular country may result in lower sales of other items which will fail to increase profits

The author of the argument may have omitted some information to make his position appear stronger. What information would help you decide if the argument has validity or what should the writer's audience know in order to make an informed decision?

Additional information needed to better evaluate the argument

a) Total sales minus cost of goods on the days of the promotions

b) Any additional incentives to buy the featured country's food

After completing these steps, you should have enough material to write your analysis. Remember that you are not creating a position of your own; you are evaluating the strengths and weaknesses of the existing argument. You do not have to include all of the points that you have created in your prewriting. In fact, during the process of drafting your analysis, other ideas may come to mind, and, if they strengthen your analysis, you should include them.

Sample Essay

The author contends that a food store will increase sales if it puts food specialties from a particular country on sale for a week while playing music from that country. This contention is supported by the experience of a wine store that sold more French wine than Italian when French music was playing, and more Italian wine than French when Italian music was playing. However, this conclusion lacks credibility as its main supporting arguments are based on faulty causation, a weak comparison and a lack of evidence.

The author's primary mistake is assuming causation regarding the driver of wine sales but failing to prove it. Specifically, the author states that the music played in the store changed the buying behavior of the customers. However, the author fails to consider or eliminate other possible causes of the increase in sales of French wine or Italian wine. For example, when French music was played, the wine store may have had the French wine on sale or may have had other promotions on French wine. The sale price or other promotions may have been the actual cause of the increased sales of wine from a particular country, rather than the fact that the store happened to be playing music from that country.

Furthermore, the author makes a faulty analogy in assuming that sales patterns that occurred at a wine store will be repeated in a food store. Food is a staple while wine is a luxury good. Customers may be less susceptible to changing their food-purchase plans than their wine-purchase plans in response to marketing promotions. As such, customers of a food store may react quite differently than customers of a wine store to promotions. Therefore, there is no reason to assume that marketing that worked in one type of shop will work in another.

Finally, the author fails to provide evidence that selling more French wine on certain days or more Italian wine on certain days will translate into more profit overall. If a company sells more French wine, it may sell less wine from other countries. Its overall profit margin would not change but only the specific type of product sold. Without the author providing evidence to show that the overall profit increased, there is no basis for arguing that the wine store increased its profits, and thus no support for the argument that the food store should emulate the wine store.

Taking into consideration the causation errors, faulty analogies and lack of evidence that playing music is a profitable marketing strategy, the author's argument lacks validity. To provide stronger support for this marketing proposal, the author would need to provide additional information on the impact of music on customer purchases in a food store, as well as on whether profit margins actually increase when people buy more products from a particular country.

Argument Task 49

> *The following appeared in a memorandum from the director of research and development at Ready-to-Ware, a software engineering firm:*
>
> *"The package of benefits and incentives that Ready-to-Ware offers to professional staff is too costly. Our quarterly profits have declined since the package was introduced two years ago, at the time of our incorporation. Moreover, the package had little positive effect, as we have had only marginal success in recruiting and training high-quality professional staff. To become more profitable again, Ready-to-Ware should, therefore, offer the reduced benefits package that was in place two years ago and use the savings to fund our current research and development initiatives."*
>
> *Discuss how well reasoned you find this argument. In your discussion be sure to analyze the line of reasoning and the use of evidence in the argument. For example, you may need to consider what questionable Assumptions unlike the thinking and what alternative explanations or counter examples might weaken the conclusion. You can also discuss what sort of evidence would strengthen or refute the argument, what changes in the argument would make it more logically sound, and what, if anything, would help you better evaluate its conclusion.*

Strategies

Argument

The directions for crafting your response include suggesting that you identify any questionable assumptions that may underlie or support the writer's conclusion. The assumptions may be stated or implied.

Assumptions

a) The benefits and incentives package has caused a decline in quarterly profits

b) The benefits and incentives package was not enough enticement to recruit and train high-quality professional staff

c) Diverting funding from the benefits package to research and development initiatives will increase company profits

d) Employees will accept the return to the reduced benefits package

To help you create your analysis of the argument, list alternative explanations for the claims made in the argument. What else may explain the events listed? What claims might someone on the opposite side of the argument make?

Alternative explanations and/or counterexamples

a) Ready-to-Ware may have encountered more competition during the two-year period

b) Ready-to-Ware's benefits package may not be as generous as benefits packages at other companies

c) There may be other reasons for new hires' being difficult to obtain and retain

d) Failure to hire and retain qualified employees may make it difficult to complete research and development initiatives

The author of the argument may have omitted some information to make his position appear stronger. What information would help you decide if the argument has validity or what should the writer's audience know in order to make an informed decision?

Additional information needed to better evaluate the argument

a) How Ready-to-Ware's benefits package compares to those of similar companies

b) Employee morale at Ready-to-Ware

c) Overall demand for the type of products sold by Ready-to-Ware

After completing these steps, you should have enough material to write your analysis. Remember that you are not creating a position of your own; you are evaluating the strengths and weaknesses of the existing argument. You do not have to include all of the points that you have created in your prewriting. In fact, during the process of drafting your analysis, other ideas may come to mind, and, if they strengthen your analysis, you should include them.

Sample Essay

The author suggests that Ready-to-Ware should reduce its benefits package in order to become more profitable. This argument is based on the assumption that the expensive benefits package is related to a decline in corporate profits, and the savings from reducing the benefits package will allow for research and development initiatives to be funded. However, by using faulty causation to support his arguments, the author fails to provide convincing evidence for reducing the benefits package.

First, the author confuses correlation with causation by assuming that profits declined because the expensive benefits package was introduced. However, other factors could have contributed to a decline in profits. An analysis of industry-wide sales, for example, may show an overall decline or Ready-to-Ware may have faced increased competition in a profitable product line. Without ruling out other causes of the decline, it cannot be assumed that the benefits package caused or contributed to a decline in profits.

Another causation error is linking the ineffectiveness of the benefits package to recruiting and training difficulties. There are many reasons why the company may be unable to recruit or train new staff. For example, the benefits package may still be insufficient compared with others in the industry or the company may not be considered to be a good place to work. The fact that the company is not able to hire the staff it needs cannot be linked to the benefits package. In fact, reducing the benefits offered may make it even more difficult to hire quality staff.

Finally, the author indicates that the reduction in the benefits package will allow the company to fund and focus on research and development efforts. In making this argument, the author makes several assumptions. The author assumes that the savings will be sufficient to fund these efforts. The author also assumes that these efforts will be able to be carried out. If the company is facing challenges in finding staff, there may be an insufficient number of qualified people to actually perform research and development. This is especially true if the company reduces its benefit package and as a result fewer employees are willing to go to work for the company.

The author takes an overly simplistic approach to his argument by applying causation instead of providing evidence for the link between the reduced benefits and decline in profitability. To support a reduction in the benefits package, solid evidence should link it to the decline in profits, and the recruiting and training challenges. Furthermore, the impact of cutting benefits on employee morale and turnover should be considered.

Argument Task 50

> *The following appeared in a memorandum from the director of marketing for a pharmaceutical company:*
>
> *"According to a survey of 5,000 urban residents, the prevalence of stress headaches increases with educational level, so that stress headaches occur most often among people with graduate-school degrees. It is well established that, nationally, higher educational levels usually correspond with higher levels of income. Therefore, in marketing our new pain remedy, Omnilixir, we should send free samples primarily to graduate students and to people with graduate degrees, and we should concentrate on advertising in professional journals rather than in general interest magazines."*
>
> *Discuss how well reasoned you find this argument. In your discussion be sure to analyze the line of reasoning and the use of evidence in the argument. For example, you may need to consider what questionable Assumptions unlike the thinking and what alternative explanations or counter examples might weaken the conclusion. You can also discuss what sort of evidence would strengthen or refute the argument, what changes in the argument would make it more logically sound, and what, if anything, would help you better evaluate its conclusion.*

Strategies

Argument

The directions for crafting your response include suggesting that you identify any questionable assumptions that may underlie or support the writer's conclusion. The assumptions may be stated or implied.

Assumptions

a) Stress contributes to a significant number of headaches

b) People with graduate-school degrees have more stress headaches than those with lower-level degrees

c) A large portion of the population has graduate-school degrees

d) Omnilixir is the most effective remedy for stress headaches

e) Sending free samples and advertising in professional journals are effective marketing strategies

f) Sales to people with graduate-level degrees will buy enough Omnilixir to ensure big profits

To help you create your analysis of the argument, list alternative explanations for the claims made in the argument. What else may explain the events listed? What claims might someone on the opposite side of the argument make?

Alternative explanations and/or counterexamples

a) People with more education may have more stressful jobs

   b)   The sample is too small to conclude that a large portion of the population has graduate degrees

   c)   Those with graduate degrees do not necessarily make higher incomes

   d)   Those who make more money don't necessarily pay more for pain relievers

   e)   People with graduate degrees may not read professional journals

   f)   Alternatives to free samples as a marketing strategy may be more effective

The author of the argument may have omitted some information to make his position appear stronger. What information would help you decide if the argument has validity or what should the writer's audience know in order to make an informed decision?

Additional information needed to better evaluate the argument

   a)   How effective free samples are as a marketing strategy

   b)   In which profession people suffer the most headaches

   c)   How the effectiveness of Omnilixir compares to that of other pain relievers

   d)   The source of advertising that most appeals to those with advanced degrees

After completing these steps, you should have enough material to write your analysis. Remember that you are not creating a position of your own; you are evaluating the strengths and weaknesses of the existing argument. You do not have to include all of the points that you have created in your prewriting. In fact, during the process of drafting your analysis, other ideas may come to mind, and, if they strengthen your analysis, you should include them.

Sample Essay

The author concludes that stress headaches increase with education levels and those with graduate-school degrees are thus more likely to have stress headaches. Because the author believes that this link exists, he suggests that advertising for a new pain relief medication should be included in professional journals to target graduate students. However, the author makes numerous faulty assumptions that render his argument unconvincing.

The first problem with the author's argument is that he makes a causation error. The author believes that people get more stress headaches because they are more educated. In fact, while there might be a correlation between higher education and stress headaches, there is no evidence that more education causes stress headaches. There are many other explanations. For example, those who have graduate degrees might work in jobs that are more likely to cause stress headaches.

Second, the author ignores any limitations of the study sample, which comprised 5,000 residents in an urban area. There is no reason to assume that all people with graduate degrees will react in the same way as those who were studied. There is also no justification for the author's singling out of people with graduate degrees, as opposed to those who have completed other types of higher-educational training. The author also fails to provide sufficient evidence or support for his statement that those who have graduate degrees are likely to make more money, and that more money is more likely to translate into the purchase of their pain medication. Many factors, including what type of graduate degree a person has, what his/her chosen profession is, what school he/she went to and what grades he/she received all go into whether a person makes more money or not. Merely having a graduate degree is not a predictor that someone will make more money, as a person in a graduate degree from a poor school or in a field where there are few jobs might make less money than someone with a bachelor's degree from a better school in a more relevant field. Further, even if someone does make more money, there is no reason to assume he/she would spend it on pain medication since there are any numbers of things a person could choose to spend money on.

Third, faulty assumptions are also used to support the suggestion to market in professional journals. The author provides no basis for assuming that those who have graduate degrees are more likely to read professional journals than general-interest magazines.

Finally, the author assumes that those who have stress headaches are the best people to target Omnilixir towards, ignoring the fact that there may be many others with headaches or painful conditions who need and may even invest more in painkillers. Limiting the advertising only to those with stress headaches is a very narrow focus for a company. Moreover, it leaves more opportunity for competitors to steal market share.

By basing the argument on the faulty premise that more education is linked to an increase in headaches, the author proceeds to create a marketing plan based on circular reasoning. Specifically, this premise leads to the false assumption that graduate students read more professional journals. To devise an effective marketing plan, first the faulty assumptions should be replaced with solid evidence of consumer buying behavior of painkillers.

Argument Task 51

> *The following appeared in a corporate planning memorandum for a company that develops amusement parks:*
>
> *"Because travel from our country to foreign countries has increased dramatically in recent years, our next project should be a 'World Tour' theme park with replicas of famous foreign buildings, rides that have international themes, and refreshment stands serving only foods from the country represented by the nearest ride. The best location would be near our capital city, which has large percentages of international residents and of children under the age of 16. Given the advantages of this site and the growing interest in foreign countries, the 'World Tour' theme park should be as successful as our space-travel theme park, where attendance has increased tenfold over the past decade."*
>
> *Discuss how well reasoned you find this argument. In your discussion be sure to analyze the line of reasoning and the use of evidence in the argument. For example, you may need to consider what questionable Assumptions unlike the thinking and what alternative explanations or counter examples might weaken the conclusion. You can also discuss what sort of evidence would strengthen or refute the argument, what changes in the argument would make it more logically sound, and what, if anything, would help you better evaluate its conclusion.*

Strategies

Argument

The directions for crafting your response include suggesting that you identify any questionable assumptions that may underlie or support the writer's conclusion. The assumptions may be stated or implied.

Assumptions

a) Increased travel to foreign countries signals an interest in theme parks featuring amusements representing foreign countries

b) The dramatic increase in foreign travel has occurred consistently over the past several years

c) International residents and children under the age of sixteen are most likely to patronize a world tour-theme amusement park

d) The success of the space-travel theme park will be duplicated at the world-tour theme park

To help you create your analysis of the argument, list alternative explanations for the claims made in the argument. What else may explain the events listed? What claims might someone on the opposite side of the argument make?

Alternative explanations and/or counterexamples

a) People who travel to foreign countries are not likely to find the experience replicated at a theme park

b) Those who travel to foreign countries may prefer an entirely different experience in a theme park

c) A space-themed amusement park offers an experience that cannot be obtained in real life for most people

The author of the argument may have omitted some information to make his position appear stronger. What information would help you decide if the argument has validity or what should the writer's audience know in order to make an informed decision?

Additional information needed to better evaluate the argument

a) The types of individuals and families that are likely to visit an amusement park

b) How frequently the capital city residents would patronize the park

After completing these steps, you should have enough material to write your analysis. Remember that you are not creating a position of your own; you are evaluating the strengths and weaknesses of the existing argument. You do not have to include all of the points that you have created in your prewriting. In fact, during the process of drafting your analysis, other ideas may come to mind, and, if they strengthen your analysis, you should include them.

Sample Essay

The author of this article suggests that a World Tour theme park should be built because of an increase in interest in foreign travel. The author believes that the World Tour theme park will be as successful as a space-travel theme park. However, this is one of several faulty analogies and assumptions that provide weak support for the proposed theme park.

The author's primary assumption is that individuals who enjoy traveling the world will enjoy visiting a theme park related to traveling the world. There are many reasons people may travel to foreign countries, including getting to see sites in person and experiencing the culture of a foreign country firsthand. These experiences cannot be replicated at a theme park, and there is no reason to believe that those who are traveling will decide to visit a theme park instead.

The author next makes the unsupported assumption that international residents and children under age 16 will be more likely to visit a World Tour theme park. There is no support or basis for this argument, other than the author's assertion that the park be located near a capital city. Many factors will influence the demographics, including location, foreign tourism and the type of entertainment offered.

Finally, the author makes a faulty analogy when suggesting that the World Tour theme park is likely to be as profitable and successful as a space-theme park. Interest in a space-theme cannot be directly compared to that in a world travel theme because many people can travel to foreign countries but traveling to space is not possible for the average person. There is no evidence to suggest that the success of a space-related theme park will be replicated or related in any way to the success of a travel-related theme park.

Because the author makes an error in assuming that traveling and visiting a theme park offer similar experiences, and fails to provide a basis for comparing a world tour park and a space theme park, the proposal for a theme park is not supported by convincing evidence.

Argument Task 52

The following appeared in a memorandum from the publisher to the staff of The Clarion, a large metropolitan newspaper:

"During the recent campaign for mayor, a clear majority of city readers who responded to our survey indicated a desire for more news about city government. To increase circulation, and thus our profits, we should therefore consistently devote a greater proportion of space in all editions of The Clarion to coverage of local news."

Discuss how well reasoned you find this argument. In your discussion be sure to analyze the line of reasoning and the use of evidence in the argument. For example, you may need to consider what questionable Assumptions unlike the thinking and what alternative explanations or counter examples might weaken the conclusion. You can also discuss what sort of evidence would strengthen or refute the argument, what changes in the argument would make it more logically sound, and what, if anything, would help you better evaluate its conclusion.

Strategies

Argument

The directions for crafting your response include suggesting that you identify any questionable assumptions that may underlie or support the writer's conclusion. The assumptions may be stated or implied.

Assumptions

a) A large number of people completed the survey

b) The questions on the survey were sufficiently representative to produce reliable results

c) Interest in news about city government will continue after the election

d) Increased circulation will lead to greater profits

e) Interest in news about city government will transfer to interest in local news of all types

f) A reduction in the proportion of space used for other than local news will not lead to a loss of readers

To help you create your analysis of the argument, list alternative explanations for the claims made in the argument. What else may explain the events listed? What claims might someone on the opposite side of the argument make?

Alternative explanations and/or counterexamples

a) Interest in local news will decline after the election

b) The sale of more newspapers has little effect on profits

c) Reducing coverage of other topics may lead to a loss of readers

The author of the argument may have omitted some information to make his position appear stronger. What

information would help you decide if the argument has validity or what should the writer's audience know in order to make an informed decision?

Additional information needed to better evaluate the argument

a) How many readers responded to the survey

b) What portion of the paper is currently devoted to local news

c) What portion of the Clarion's profit is created by newspaper sales

After completing these steps, you should have enough material to write your analysis. Remember that you are not creating a position of your own; you are evaluating the strengths and weaknesses of the existing argument. You do not have to include all of the points that you have created in your prewriting. In fact, during the process of drafting your analysis, other ideas may come to mind, and, if they strengthen your analysis, you should include them.

Sample Essay

The author concludes that The Clarion should cover more local news in order to increase its subscriber base. The author's basis for this argument is the results of a survey of city readers during a mayoral campaign. Unfortunately, the proposed local news strategy is subject to several limitations, including the use of unrepresentative data and the over generalization of past trends. Consequently, it relies on several false assumptions to conclude that increasing local news coverage is the best option for increasing circulation and profits.

The first problem with the author's argument is that it assumes that the results of a voluntary study conducted by city readers are reflective of what the people as a whole want. There is, however, nothing to suggest that the opinions of a few survey respondents are reflective of the needs and desires of the people as a whole. In fact, the results may be skewed by the profile of the respondents. The number of readers who responded may have been small and limited to those who were already subscribers. And those with an interest in politics and the election may have been more likely to respond. If others in the area do not agree with the opinion provided on the survey, they will not subscribe and neither circulation nor profits will increase.

Second, the author over generalizes by assuming that the desire to read more about a city election during a mayoral race translates into a general interest in local news at all times. The survey respondents may have been interested in local government only because of the political race going on at the time. They may have been drawn into the election politics by specific issues and the marketing campaigns of candidates. There is no evidence that non-regular readers will continue to read the paper, find general local news to be equally interesting or subscribe to read this general news.

Finally, drawing on incomplete information and faulty logic, the author makes an assumption that covering local news will increase circulation and, in turn, increase profits. There is no evidence to support this cause-effect relationship. Other subscribers who are not interested in local news may stop their subscriptions. There is insufficient information provided to determine that those who are not subscribers already will become subscribers.

By ignoring the fact that the survey sample was limited and took place when a political race was going on, the author makes many unsupported assumptions about the readers and potential readers of the newspaper. The study results may not be an accurate measure of the desires of the wider population as a whole. The author's argument cannot be relied upon without further research into the profile and interests of potential subscribers in the area.

Argument Task 53

> *The following appeared as part of the business plan of the Capital Idea investment firm:*
>
> "*Across town in the Park Hill district, the Thespian Theater, Pizzazz Pizza, and the Niblick Golf Club have all had business increases over the past two years. Capital Idea should therefore invest in the Roxy Playhouse, the Slice-o'-Pizza, and the Divot Golf Club, three new businesses in the Irongate district. As a condition, we should require them to participate in a special program: Any customer who patronizes two of the businesses will receive a substantial discount at the third. By motivating customers to patronize all three, we will thus contribute to the profitability of each and maximize our return.*"
>
> *Discuss how well reasoned you find this argument. In your discussion be sure to analyze the line of reasoning and the use of evidence in the argument. For example, you may need to consider what questionable Assumptions unlike the thinking and what alternative explanations or counter examples might weaken the conclusion. You can also discuss what sort of evidence would strengthen or refute the argument, what changes in the argument would make it more logically sound, and what, if anything, would help you better evaluate its conclusion.*

Strategies

Argument

The directions for crafting your response include suggesting that you identify any questionable assumptions that may underlie or support the writer's conclusion. The assumptions may be stated or implied.

Assumptions

a) The type of businesses that have been successful in the Park Hill district will be successful in the Irongate district

b) The new businesses will be receptive to Capital Idea's condition for its investment in them

c) The discounts will be shared equally among the three businesses

d) A large number of customers will patronize all three businesses

e) Sales volume will compensate for the discounts so the businesses will be profitable

To help you create your analysis of the argument, list alternative explanations for the claims made in the argument. What else may explain the events listed? What claims might someone on the opposite side of the argument make?

Alternative explanations and/or counterexamples

a) The demographics of each district may support different types of businesses

b) People may not patronize all three businesses equally

c) Discounts may cut into profits too deeply for all three businesses to survive

The author of the argument may have omitted some information to make his position appear stronger. What information would help you decide if the argument has validity or what should the writer's audience know in order to make an informed decision?

Additional information needed to better evaluate the argument

a) Ethnic and economic composition of the population in the Irongate district

After completing these steps, you should have enough material to write your analysis. Remember that you are not creating a position of your own; you are evaluating the strengths and weaknesses of the existing argument. You do not have to include all of the points that you have created in your prewriting. In fact, during the process of drafting your analysis, other ideas may come to mind, and, if they strengthen your analysis, you should include them.

Sample Essay

The author of this argument encourages investing in three new businesses opening in the Irongate district based on the performance of similar businesses in the Park Hill district. By relying on faulty assumptions and analogies to make this argument, the author fails to make a convincing case for the investments.

The major problem with the author's argument is it is based on a faulty analogy between business results in the Park Hill district and those in the Irongate district. There is nothing to suggest that these districts are related or correlated in any way, so the success of businesses in one district may have nothing to do with the success of those in another district. For example, the demographics of one district may be young upper middle class theatre goers while the other district may have a higher percentage of retired golf enthusiasts. Thus, sales and the success of discount programs would vary among the businesses. Further, the past success of specific businesses is not a guarantee of future success.

The author's recommendation that the businesses should be marketed by offering a discount to customers who visit three businesses is also unsupported and problematic. First, the author assumes that the third business would be willing to provide a discount, and could do so profitably. There is no reason to believe that a business would be willing to substantially lower its prices simply because a customer supported two other businesses in a similar geographic area. These customers may not represent a key target market or level of revenue per customer. Nor is there any evidence to show that customers will be interested in visiting the third business.

Further, offering this substantial discount might undercut profit for all businesses. This is the opposite of the author's aim to maximize returns and contribute to the profitability of all businesses. Unless the author could show that the money lost by offering a discount would be recovered due to an increase in the number of visitors to all three locations, then there is no reason to believe that a discount would increase profits.

The author fails to consider many relevant factors and instead draws on faulty analogies and causation, including a weak correlation between business success in two different cities. To assess the viability of the three new businesses, research should be conducted on the demographics and business drivers in Irongate.

Argument Task 54

The following appeared in a memorandum from the marketing department of a children's clothing manufacturer:

"Our HuggyBunny brand is the bestselling brand of children's clothing. Parents everywhere recognize the HuggyBunny logo as a mark of quality, and most parents are likely to buy children's clothes with the familiar HuggyBunny brand and logo than otherwise identical clothes without it. Therefore, if we use the HuggyBunny brand name and logo for the new line of clothing for teenagers that our company will soon be introducing, that clothing will sell better than it would if we labeled it with a new brand name and logo."

Discuss how well reasoned you find this argument. In your discussion be sure to analyze the line of reasoning and the use of evidence in the argument. For example, you may need to consider what questionable Assumptions unlike the thinking and what alternative explanations or counter examples might weaken the conclusion. You can also discuss what sort of evidence would strengthen or refute the argument, what changes in the argument would make it more logically sound, and what, if anything, would help you better evaluate its conclusion.

Strategies

Argument

The directions for crafting your response include suggesting that you identify any questionable assumptions that may underlie or support the writer's conclusion. The assumptions may be stated or implied.

Assumptions

a) Parents of teenagers rather than teenagers themselves buy teen clothing

b) Teens will have the same regard for the HuggyBunny brand and logo that their parents do.

c) The same marketing strategy that works for parents of young children will work for teenagers

d) Parents buy the HuggyBunny brand for its high quality

To help you create your analysis of the argument, list alternative explanations for the claims made in the argument. What else may explain the events listed? What claims might someone on the opposite side of the argument make?

Alternative explanations and/or counterexamples

a) Parents may buy the HuggyBunny brand because it is widely available or costs less than other brands

b) Teens are not likely to desire clothing with the same label and name as the clothing they wore when they were young children

The author of the argument may have omitted some information to make his position appear stronger. What

information would help you decide if the argument has validity or what should the writer's audience know in order to make an informed decision?

Additional information needed to better evaluate the argument

   a)   Evidence that parents buy HuggyBunny because of the brand's high quality merchandise

After completing these steps, you should have enough material to write your analysis. Remember that you are not creating a position of your own; you are evaluating the strengths and weaknesses of the existing argument. You do not have to include all of the points that you have created in your prewriting. In fact, during the process of drafting your analysis, other ideas may come to mind, and, if they strengthen your analysis, you should include them.

Sample Essay

The author of this argument indicates that parents buy HuggyBunny clothing for their children because of the HuggyBunny brand and logo. Because the brand is recognized among parents of children, the author recommends using the same brand name and logo on clothing produced for teenagers. Unfortunately, the author makes several logical errors in evaluating the buying behaviors of parents and teens, resulting in a flawed marketing strategy for teens.

The author's first error is in assuming that HuggyBunny's sales reports are representative of the buying behavior of all consumers. Although sales reports may show that parents are likely to buy kids clothing with HuggyBunny's logo on it, these sales reports may be limited only to a specific group of parents. The characteristics and thus choices of a small group may not represent those of the broader population. Without further information on how representative the information in the sales reports is, a viable marketing strategy cannot be developed from its conclusions.

Second, the author makes the assumption that it is the HuggyBunny brand name and logo that causes parents to choose their clothing. This faulty correlation ignores other factors that may be encouraging parents to buy HuggyBunny. For example, because HuggyBunny is a best seller, it may be more widely available and parents may buy it because it is convenient. Thus, further research is required to determine the factors underlying the buying behavior of parents.

Finally, the author makes an assumption that teenagers who are looking for clothing, or that parents who buy clothing for teenagers, will be familiar with and swayed by the HuggyBunny name. This argument is also based on a weak correlation. The market for clothing for teens is very different than the market for kid's clothing. There is no reason to assume that teens and people who buy for teens are even familiar with HuggyBunny. If the teens are familiar with HuggyBunny, these teens may be less likely to purchase clothing seen as childish, although the author does not acknowledge this possibility.

By erroneously assuming that parents of young kids will have the same buying behavior as teens, the author develops a marketing strategy based on weak correlations. He fails to support the assumptions that HuggyBunny's sales figures represent the needs of the population as a whole, and teenagers will look for the same brand as parents buying clothing for children. Since neither the initial premise that parents are drawn to the HuggyBunny brand name nor the related assumptions are supported, the author's branding strategy for teenage clothing is flawed.

Argument Task 55

> The following appeared in a memorandum written by the managing director of the Exeunt Theater Company:
>
> "Now that we have moved to a larger theater, we can expect to increase our revenues from ticket sales. To further increase profits, we should start producing the plays that have been most successful when they were performed in our nation's largest cities. In addition, we should hire the Adlib Theater Company's director of fund-raising, since corporate contributions to Adlib have increased significantly over the three years that she has worked for Adlib."
>
> Discuss how well reasoned you find this argument. In your discussion be sure to analyze the line of reasoning and the use of evidence in the argument. For example, you may need to consider what questionable Assumptions unlike the thinking and what alternative explanations or counter examples might weaken the conclusion. You can also discuss what sort of evidence would strengthen or refute the argument, what changes in the argument would make it more logically sound, and what, if anything, would help you better evaluate its conclusion.

Strategies

Argument

The directions for crafting your response include suggesting that you identify any questionable assumptions that may underlie or support the writer's conclusion. The assumptions may be stated or implied.

Assumptions

a) More people will attend the performances because the company has moved to a larger theater

b) Plays that have been successful in the nation's largest cities will be successful in the city where the Exeunt Theater Company performs

c) Hiring Adlib Theater Company's director of fund-raising will increase corporate contributions to Exeunt Theater Company

d) Increased ticket sales will lead to greater profits

To help you create your analysis of the argument, list alternative explanations for the claims made in the argument. What else may explain the events listed? What claims might someone on the opposite side of the argument make?

Alternative explanations and/or counterexamples

a) The cost of operating a larger theater will offset increase revenues from ticket sales

b) There are few corporations to provide donations for Exeunt eliminating the necessity to hire someone to work on that

The author of the argument may have omitted some information to make his position appear stronger. What

information would help you decide if the argument has validity or what should the writer's audience know in order to make an informed decision?

Additional information needed to better evaluate the argument

a) How many people are unable to get tickets for productions in the current facility

b) The types of productions that are successful in small towns

After completing these steps, you should have enough material to write your analysis. Remember that you are not creating a position of your own; you are evaluating the strengths and weaknesses of the existing argument. You do not have to include all of the points that you have created in your prewriting. In fact, during the process of drafting your analysis, other ideas may come to mind, and, if they strengthen your analysis, you should include them.

Sample Essay

The author concludes that a move to a larger theater by the Exeunt Theatre Company will result in more revenue from ticket sales, and producing plays that have performed well in other cities will further increase those sales. The author also argues that the theater company should hire a director of fund-raising from the Adlib Theater Company since donations have increased during the director's tenure with Adlib.

The author makes several faulty assumptions in making his argument. The first is a causation error, assuming that a larger theater will translate to more revenue from ticket sales. However, it is not the size of the theater but the quality of the entertainment that will cause people to buy tickets. If the plays are not popular with the public and worse receive negative reviews from critics, then ticket sales will be poor. To correct this causation error, Exeunt should focus on the quality and popularity of plays performed in smaller cities.

Second, the author uses a faulty analogy to show that a play which is successful in a large city will be well received at the Exeunt Theater Company. There is no evidence to suggest that the people located near the Exeunt Theater will respond in the same way as people did in the nation's largest cities. Furthermore, theatre in larger cities can afford higher paid talent and more elaborate costumes and sets, which can contribute to a play's success. Since no relationship is shown between successful theatre in large and small cities, the Exeunt Theatre should focus on identifying the success factors of plays in smaller cities.

Finally, the author makes a causation error when stating that the Adlib Theater Company's director should be hired as a result of the increase in corporate contributions to Adlib during her time of working for Adlib. However, there are many possible reasons for the increase in donations and the author fails to provide evidence that the main reason was because of the director. For example, there may be a strong corporate donor base supporting Adlib and there may not be as many- or any - corporations in the smaller city.

More favorable tax deductions on charitable donations could have increased donations to the arts. In fact, there is no evidence to indicate that the Exeunt Theater Company will experience the same fundraising benefits that the Adlib Company did, regardless of whether they hire the director.

The author, therefore, makes a weak argument based on faulty analogies and causation errors. To develop a viable theatre strategy for Exeunt, the author would need to provide support for the assertion that ticket sales will increase, as well as evidence that the plays proposed would do well locally. Finally, the author would need to establish a link between the director's fundraising efforts and the increased fundraising capability of Adlib Company, and further prove that Exeunt could also increase its fundraising if Adlib's director were hired.

Argument Task 56

> *The following appeared as part of a business plan by the Capital Idea investment firm:*
>
> *"In recent years the worldwide demand for fish has grown, and improvements in fishing technology have made larger catches and thus increased supply possible: for example, last year's tuna catch was 9 percent greater than the previous year's. To capitalize on these trends, we should therefore invest in the new tartfish processing plant on Tartfish Island, where increasing revenues from tourism indicate a strong local economy."*
>
> *Discuss how well reasoned you find this argument. In your discussion be sure to analyze the line of reasoning and the use of evidence in the argument. For example, you may need to consider what questionable Assumptions unlike the thinking and what alternative explanations or counter examples might weaken the conclusion. You can also discuss what sort of evidence would strengthen or refute the argument, what changes in the argument would make it more logically sound, and what, if anything, would help you better evaluate its conclusion.*

Strategies

Argument

The directions for crafting your response include suggesting that you identify any questionable assumptions that may underlie or support the writer's conclusion. The assumptions may be stated or implied.

Assumptions

   a)   Improvements in fishing technology are responsible for the increased tuna catch

   b)   A 9 percent increase in the tuna catch is significant

   c)   The worldwide demand for fish will make the demand for Tartfish increase

   d)   The worldwide demand for fish will continue to rise

   e)   A strong economy related to tourism makes investing in the processing plant on Tartfish Island a good idea

To help you create your analysis of the argument, list alternative explanations for the claims made in the argument. What else may explain the events listed? What claims might someone on the opposite side of the argument make?

Alternative explanations and/or counterexamples

   a)   There has been an increase in the number of boats fishing for tuna

   b)   Tartfish do not have the popularity of other types of fish

   c)   The previous year's tuna catch was lower than normal

The author of the argument may have omitted some information to make his position appear stronger. What

information would help you decide if the argument has validity or what should the writer's audience know in order to make an informed decision?

Additional information needed to better evaluate the argument

a) If the demand for fish has increased steadily

b) The reason for the increased demand for fish

c) How last year's tuna catch compared to other years' catches

After completing these steps, you should have enough material to write your analysis. Remember that you are not creating a position of your own; you are evaluating the strengths and weaknesses of the existing argument. You do not have to include all of the points that you have created in your prewriting. In fact, during the process of drafting your analysis, other ideas may come to mind, and, if they strengthen your analysis, you should include them.

Sample Essay

In this argument, the author suggests that demand for fish has grown and the ability to catch fish has increased, making now a prime time to capitalize on trends in fishing. The author's suggestion for capitalizing on this worldwide increase in fishing is to open a new tartfish processing plant on Tartfish Island. Unfortunately, this author's argument falls apart when considered carefully since the author makes many unsupported assumptions.

A major problem with this author's argument is that the author assumes that worldwide demand for fish will continue to grow and that the supply of fish will continue to grow as well. It is impossible to determine the accuracy of this assumption without further information about what drove the increased demand and about whether the increase in demand is outpacing the increase in supply. If demand is increasing at a more rapid pace than the ability to catch fish, then the supply may soon be exhausted. On the other hand, if demand increased only temporarily, then the demand may fall off in the future.

Another issue with the author's argument is that the author attempts to analogize a worldwide increase in the supply and demand of fish with an increase of a particular type of fish in a particular location. Just because the worldwide demand for fish increased and because the catches of some type of fish (tuna) have increased does not mean that either supply or demand of tartfish will increase or that the trend of increased demand will exist on Tartfish Island.

Finally, the author assumes that revenues from tourism indicate a strong local economy. Without further information, the author cannot automatically assume the link between tourism and the local economy.

Because the author makes unsupported assumptions and fails to fully understand the actual implications of worldwide trends on fish, the author's argument is not supported by the information he provides. Further information would thus be necessary to determine if tartfish demand is increasing or if a tartfish processing plant would be a wise investment.

Argument Task 57

> *The following appeared in a memorandum from the business planning department of Avia Airlines:*
>
> *"Of all the cities in their region, Beaumont and Fletcher are showing the fastest growth in the number of new businesses. Therefore, Avia should establish a commuter route between them as a means of countering recent losses on its main passenger routes. And to make the commuter route more profitable from the outset, Avia should offer a 1/3 discount on tickets purchased within two days of the flight. Unlike tickets bought earlier, discount tickets will be nonrefundable, and so gain from their sale will be greater"*
>
> *Discuss how well reasoned you find this argument. In your discussion be sure to analyze the line of reasoning and the use of evidence in the argument. For example, you may need to consider what questionable Assumptions unlike the thinking and what alternative explanations or counter examples might weaken the conclusion. You can also discuss what sort of evidence would strengthen or refute the argument, what changes in the argument would make it more logically sound, and what, if anything, would help you better evaluate its conclusion.*

Strategies

Argument

The directions for crafting your response include suggesting that you identify any questionable assumptions that may underlie or support the writer's conclusion. The assumptions may be stated or implied.

Assumptions

   a) There will be enough passengers on a commuter route between Beaumont and Fletcher to compensate for Avia's losses on its main passenger routes

   b) Growth in the number of new businesses in Beaumont and Fletcher will create a demand for a new commuter route

   c) Enough commuters will fail to use the nonrefundable discount tickets to make the new commuter route profitable

To help you create your analysis of the argument, list alternative explanations for the claims made in the argument. What else may explain the events listed? What claims might someone on the opposite side of the argument make?

Alternative explanations and/or counterexamples

   a) A majority of workers in the businesses live nearby and do not commute a great distance to work

   b) The new businesses may enable employees to work online and eliminate the need to commute to work

    c)   Commuters will be reluctant to purchase nonrefundable tickets, eliminating the possibility of higher ticket sales

    d)   The new growth simply offsets the closing of other businesses

The author of the argument may have omitted some information to make his position appear stronger. What information would help you decide if the argument has validity or what should the writer's audience know in order to make an informed decision?

Additional information needed to better evaluate the argument

    a)   How much commuter traffic will be generated by new businesses in the two cities

    b)   The net growth in the number of businesses

After completing these steps, you should have enough material to write your analysis. Remember that you are not creating a position of your own; you are evaluating the strengths and weaknesses of the existing argument. You do not have to include all of the points that you have created in your prewriting. In fact, during the process of drafting your analysis, other ideas may come to mind, and, if they strengthen your analysis, you should include them.

Sample Essay

The author suggests that Avia Airlines should establish a route between Beaumont and Fletcher because these cities are showing the fastest growth in the number of new businesses. The author also suggests Avia offer discounts on tickets purchased within two days of the flight and make those tickets nonrefundable in order to increase profits. However, in making these arguments, the author uses faulty causality, and therefore builds the case for the two new commuter routes on unproven assumptions instead of solid evidence.

First, the author applies faulty causality by concluding that Avia Airlines should establish a route between Beaumont and Fletcher because these cities are showing the fastest growth in the number of new businesses. However, this does not necessarily mean that they actually have the most businesses or best economies. They may be showing fast growth because they had the least number of developed businesses. If this were the case, then other areas with more established businesses may actually have more business activity and potential commuter traffic for Avia.

Second, the author assumes a link between business growth and activity, and the need for a commuter airline or commuter route. Some businesses, however, may not produce commuter traffic, such as the fast growing online business sector. Without evidence to support the author's implied suggestion that more businesses means more commuting from location to location, there is no reason to believe that increased business activity leads to a demand for a commuter flight.

Finally, the proposal to offer discounted tickets and make those tickets nonrefundable is also based on problematic assumptions. First, the author assumes that the discount provided on tickets purchased within days of the trip will entice enough additional people to buy tickets that it will make up for the cost of the discount. There is no evidence to suggest this, especially since there is no reason to assume that business travelers will have the flexibility to make last-minute travel plans.

Moreover, the author fails to show that making discounted tickets non-refundable will increase the company's profit. Instead, people may be reluctant to buy these non-refundable tickets due to the inability to receive a refund. Many other undisclosed factors affecting ticket sales need to be considered, including the size of the discount, the policy regarding transferring to other dates, and the number of available flights.

By applying faulty causality, the author's arguments in support of new commuter lines for Avia are weak and cannot be relied upon. The causal relationships used to support key facts are not convincing and have failed to hold up against logical reasoning. To present a viable proposal for new commuter lines, the author should provide evidence that the increase in business in a city has created a verifiable need for a commuter line, and that the new route and related promotions such as discounted tickets can operate profitably.

Argument Task 58

> *The following appeared in a memorandum to the work-group supervisors of the GBS Company:*
>
> *"The CoffeeCart beverage and food service located in the lobby of our main office building is not earning enough in sales to cover its costs, and so the cart may discontinue operating at GBS. Given the low staff morale, as evidenced by the increase in the number of employees leaving the company, the loss of this service could present a problem, especially since the staff morale questionnaire showed widespread dissatisfaction with the snack machines. Therefore, supervisors should remind the employees in their group to patronize the cart—after all; it was leased for their convenience so that they would not have to walk over to the cafeteria on breaks."*
>
> *Discuss how well reasoned you find this argument. In your discussion be sure to analyze the line of reasoning and the use of evidence in the argument. For example, you may need to consider what questionable Assumptions unlike the thinking and what alternative explanations or counter examples might weaken the conclusion. You can also discuss what sort of evidence would strengthen or refute the argument, what changes in the argument would make it more logically sound, and what, if anything, would help you better evaluate its conclusion.*

Strategies

Argument

The directions for crafting your response include suggesting that you identify any questionable assumptions that may underlie or support the writer's conclusion. The assumptions may be stated or implied.

Assumptions

   a)   Employees are leaving the company because of low staff morale

   b)   Dissatisfaction with the snack machines has contributed to low staff morale

   c)   Going to the cafeteria on breaks is an inconvenience

   d)   The snack cart has items that appeal to a majority of GBS employees

To help you create your analysis of the argument, list alternative explanations for the claims made in the argument. What else may explain the events listed? What claims might someone on the opposite side of the argument make?

Alternative explanations and/or counterexamples

   a)   Employees are leaving the company because of better opportunities elsewhere

   b)   Low staff morale is caused by poor working conditions within the company

   c)   Staff may be choosing the cafeteria because it has a better selection of snacks

    d)   CoffeeCart prices are too high

The author of the argument may have omitted some information to make his position appear stronger. What information would help you decide if the argument has validity or what should the writer's audience know in order to make an informed decision?

Additional information needed to better evaluate the argument

    a)   Why people are leaving the company

    b)   How prices of the CoffeeCart compare to those in the cafeteria

After completing these steps, you should have enough material to write your analysis. Remember that you are not creating a position of your own; you are evaluating the strengths and weaknesses of the existing argument. You do not have to include all of the points that you have created in your prewriting. In fact, during the process of drafting your analysis, other ideas may come to mind, and, if they strengthen your analysis, you should include them.

Sample Essay

The author argues that a CoffeeCart beverage and food center in danger of closing could have a negative effect on employee morale. He therefore suggests that supervisors should encourage employees to use the CoffeeCart. However, the author presents an unconvincing argument by relying on faulty causation to show a relationship between low CoffeeCart sales, and low employee morale and high employee turnover.

The author makes the assumption that the CoffeeCart is struggling because people are choosing not to buy from it. However, the author does not provide proof that this is the cause of the low sales. The CoffeeCart may not offer an attractive food and beverage selection, and therefore even requiring employees to patronize it may not raise the revenue per person to sufficient levels. Moreover, there may simply not be enough people in the building to provide the CoffeeCart with enough customers, especially since more employees are leaving the company.

The author once again applies faulty causation when assuming that low morale is causing staff to leave. It cannot be assumed that it is because of low morale without other evidence. There may be many reasons why employees are leaving the company. An offer of higher wages in a competitive labor market would have a much stronger influence on job turnover than dissatisfaction with coffee cart goods or service.

Finally, the author makes yet another unproven assumption when he suggests that the dissatisfaction with snack machines is a cause or contributing factor to low employee morale. Although employees expressed in a questionnaire that they did not like the snack machines, this factor would have to be ranked among other employee satisfaction measures to weigh its impact on employee morale. The poor snack machines may be of minor concern or no concern at all and other more important factors may be the cause of the low employee morale.

By using faulty causality to explain low sales at the CoffeeCart, the author creates a chain of circular reasoning that leads to the illogical conclusion that the lack of satisfaction with the coffee cart has led to low morale which has, in turn, contributed to employee turnover. To identify the real reasons behind low CoffeeCart sales and high employee turnover, the author must replace assumptions about the behaviors and attitudes of the employees with solid facts.

Argument Task 59

> *The following appeared as part of an article in a trade magazine:*
>
> *"During a recent trial period in which government inspections at selected meat-processing plants were more frequent, the amount of bacteria in samples of processed chicken decreased by 50 percent on average from the previous year's level. If the government were to institute more frequent inspections, the incidence of stomach and intestinal infections throughout the country could thus be cut in half. In the meantime, consumers of Excel Meats should be safe from infection because Excel's main processing plant has shown more improvement in eliminating bacterial contamination than any other plant cited in the government report."*
>
> *Discuss how well reasoned you find this argument. In your discussion be sure to analyze the line of reasoning and the use of evidence in the argument. For example, you may need to consider what questionable Assumptions unlike the thinking and what alternative explanations or counter examples might weaken the conclusion. You can also discuss what sort of evidence would strengthen or refute the argument, what changes in the argument would make it more logically sound, and what, if anything, would help you better evaluate its conclusion.*

Strategies

Argument

The directions for crafting your response include suggesting that you identify any questionable assumptions that may underlie or support the writer's conclusion. The assumptions may be stated or implied.

Assumptions

a)   More frequent inspections at meat-processing plants caused a 50% reduction in bacteria in processed chicken

b)   The previous year's rate of bacteria in processed chicken was dangerously high

c)   More frequent inspections will reduce the incidence of stomach and intestinal infections throughout the country to half its current level

d)   At least half of the stomach and intestinal infections throughout the country are caused by bacteria in processed chicken

e)   Because Excel's main processing plant has shown more improvement in eliminating bacterial contamination than any other plant cited in the government report, consumers of Excel Meats should be safe from infection

f)   Excel's improvement is much greater than that in other processing plants

To help you create your analysis of the argument, list alternative explanations for the claims made in the argument. What else may explain the events listed? What claims might someone on the opposite side of the argument make?

Alternative explanations and/or counterexamples

a) Improved technology may have made eliminating bacteria possible

b) There are any numbers of causes of bacterial infections not related to meat processing

c) One year's decline in bacterial infections does not predict the rates of infection for ensuing years

d) Excel Meats may have had more room for improvement than other processing plants

The author of the argument may have omitted some information to make his position appear stronger. What information would help you decide if the argument has validity or what should the writer's audience know in order to make an informed decision?

Additional information needed to better evaluate the argument

a) How many cases of intestinal infection are caused by contaminated meat

b) How Excel Meat's rate of contamination compares to other meat processing plants

After completing these steps, you should have enough material to write your analysis. Remember that you are not creating a position of your own; you are evaluating the strengths and weaknesses of the existing argument. You do not have to include all of the points that you have created in your prewriting. In fact, during the process of drafting your analysis, other ideas may come to mind, and, if they strengthen your analysis, you should include them.

Sample Essay

The author of this argument indicates that bacteria in samples of processed chicken decreased during a period of heightened government inspections. Based on this fact, the author suggests that increasing the rate of inspection would decrease the rate of stomach and intestinal infections. The author also advises that people eat at Excel Meats because their plant has shown more improvement than others in eliminating bacterial contamination. However, the author applies faulty causation in making these arguments that fail to stand up to logical reasoning, and thus undermine the strength of his position.

In the author's first correlation/causation error, the author assumes, without supporting the assumption that a decrease in bacteria in meat processing plants was caused by government inspections. Without further evidence, however, it cannot be determined that this was the cause. Meat processing plants may have decreased the bacteria for any number of reasons including improvements in technology or health and safety practices. The author's assumption, especially based on only one year of prior data, cannot serve as the basis for a solid argument. Further, a past reduction in bacteria as a result of inspections would not necessarily guarantee the same result in the future.

The author's assertion that stomach and intestinal infections should decrease by 50 percent is also problematic. This assertion is based on the fact that the author believes inspections will reduce bacteria in meat processing plants by 50 percent. However, stomach and intestinal infections can be caused by other factors unrelated to contaminated meat. Therefore, if the rate of bacteria in meat processing plants was reduced by 50 percent, the infection rate in people would not automatically decrease by the same percentage.

Finally, the author's suggestion that people purchase from Excel Meats because they have shown the most improvement of plants cited by the government is based on a faulty and dangerous assumption. While the plant may have shown the most improvement of those cited, it may still not be as clean as other meat processing facilities that were never cited at all. It cannot and should not be assumed that Excel is the safest without knowing more about whether other plants avoided citations entirely.

Because the author makes unsupported assumptions and draws conclusions not fully supported by the facts, the author's argument is weak and should not be trusted.

Argument Task 60

> *The following appeared in the editorial section of a local newspaper:*
>
> *"This city should be able to improve existing services and provide new ones without periodically raising the taxes of the residents. Instead, the city should require that the costs of services be paid for by developers who seek approval for their large new building projects. After all, these projects can be highly profitable to the developers, but they canal so raise a city's expenses and increase the demand for its services."*
>
> *Discuss how well reasoned you find this argument. In your discussion be sure to analyze the line of reasoning and the use of evidence in the argument. For example, you may need to consider what questionable Assumptions underlie the thinking and what alternative explanations or counter examples might weaken the conclusion. You can also discuss what sort of evidence would strengthen or refute the argument, what changes in the argument would make it more logically sound, and what, if anything, would help you better evaluate its conclusion.*

Strategies

Argument

Because developers make money on their projects and the new developments increase the demand for services, developers should be required to pay for the improvement of existing services and the creation of new services.

Assumptions

a) The city is not able to improve existing services and provide new services without raising the taxes of the residents.

b) The city raises taxes in order to provide new or existing services.

c) The city has the authority or power to require that developers pay for the cost of services seeking approval.

d) Developers have the funds and willingness to pay for existing and new services

e) The new developments do not increase the tax base, making it possible for the city to provide improvements without raising taxes.

f) The developers do not pay taxes to the city already that cover the cost of any expenses the city bears due to their development.

g) Developers should be obligated to pay if their projects increase the demand for city services

h) Residents should not be required to pay for the services that they use.

i) Services provided to residents cost more to provide if there is increased demand for those services.

Sample Essay

The author of this argument believes that because developers make money on projects, and because these projects increase the demand for city services, developers should be obligated to pay the cost of providing new and existing services rather than increasing the tax burden on residents. Unfortunately, this argument makes several faulty and hidden assumptions that undermine its validity. Upon closer examination of these assumptions, the author fails to provide adequate support for the premise that developers increase the use of city services and thus should be obligated to pay for them.

The first assumption is not valid because it applies faulty causality. Specifically, it states that the government raises taxes to pay for services used by residents. It further assumes that more development means more residents who will require more services and thus more taxes will be levied. This argument fails to consider that the government may raise taxes for reasons unrelated to the use of public services by residents, such as inflation or changes in tax policy. If the tax increases are not related to the use of services by residents, then there would be no basis for imposing an obligation on developers alone to pay for the government spending funded by the tax dollars.

Even if the author is correct in assuming that the increase in tax revenues is necessary due to the increased use of government services, the author's suggestion that developers should pay is premised on hidden assumptions. First, it assumes that the city has the authority to require the developers to pay for new and existing services, which is not necessarily the case. Moreover, more information would need to be provided on whether the city even has the ability to impose this requirement.

A number of other faulty assumptions have been drawn to rationalize why the developer should pay. The author assumes that developers would have the funds to pay for the necessary services, be willing to bear these costs and earn profits that would exceed the cost of providing such services. However, if their profits do not exceed the cost of providing such services, developers will decline to develop in the area and progress will stop. The government might then be forced to provide more of the services the developers were previously providing, such as building housing areas. The added cost of the government assuming the role vacated by the developers could impose an even larger burden on taxpayers.

The author's argument also assumes that any increased use of city services will actually increase the cost in excess of the additional income to the city provided as a result of the development. However, some of the services funded by tax dollars will not become more expensive, or may become only slightly more expensive, if more people are using them as a result of new development. On the other hand, developers may pay for a building permit and pay taxes on the cost of land, while new development may increase the number of people in a location and thus increase the tax base. The income provided to the city because of the new development may more-than-outweigh the additional cost of providing new or existing services to more people.

Finally, it is possible to argue that residents should pay for the cost of the services that they are using. Residents are privileged to live in a society in which they can make use of public parks and are protected by public service professionals. Therefore, there may not be justification for requiring a developer to pay for these services provided to, and enjoyed by, the public.

Made in the USA
Lexington, KY
26 June 2017